ideal
ID7140

GRADES
1-3

FACTS in a Flash
Addition & Subtraction

Strategies for Fast Fact Recall

By
Patricia Cartland Noble

Art Director: Sara Mordecai
Cover and Page Design: Sara Mordecai
Production Design: Piper Brown
Illustrations: Duane Bibby
Editor: Jill Osofsky
Project Coordinator: Judy Crum

ISBN: 1-56451-328-9
Facts in a Flash: Addition & Subtraction, Grades 1 - 3
©2000 Ideal School Supply
A Division of Instructional Fair Group, Inc.
A Tribune Education Company
3195 Wilson Drive NW, Grand Rapids, MI 49544 • USA
Duke Street, Wisbech, Cambs, PE13 2AE • UK

All Rights Reserved • Printed in USA

Limited Reproduction Permission: Permission to duplicate these materials is limited to the teacher or parent for whom they are purchased. Reproduction for an entire school or school district is unlawful and strictly prohibited.

Contents

Introduction	3
Getting Started	5
Addition Facts Strategies	5
Subtraction Facts Strategies	14
Using the Facts Cards	17
Addition Facts Table	18
Addition Activity Pages	19
Subtraction Activity Pages	38
Addition Facts Cards	48
Subtraction Facts Cards	50
Cumulative Review: Addition	52
Cumulative Review: Subtraction	53
Mixed Review	54
Turnaround Facts Review	55
Oral Addition Facts Review	56
Oral Subtraction Facts Review	57
Selected Solutions	58

Introduction

Facts in a Flash is a collection of meaningful and fun activities that can help your students develop fluency in basic addition and subtraction facts. The book introduces different strategies children can use to think about and learn the facts.

Each strategy makes learning facts a sense-making endeavor, presenting the facts in a way that helps children understand and retain them. Each group of facts is introduced using models, pictures, and thinking aloud. Number concepts such as the commutative property, compensation, and place value are explored in place of rote memorization. The facts are grouped by strategies.

The activities are outlined in a suggested order. It is recommended that students demonstrate mastery of one strategy group before moving on to the next. This ensures that they will focus on a small group of new facts at one time. Doing so will build students' confidence, as they practice at their own pace and move on when they are ready.

Students may be introduced to a strategy during a whole class lesson, but some may need more review than others before moving on. Because students will progress through the strategies at different paces, it is important to differentiate instruction and practice whenever possible. Consider pairing students or having small groups review a strategy or extend skills as needed.

A manipulative or visual aid is used to introduce each strategy. Blackline masters for each strategy lesson are provided for practice of each set of facts. Some of the blackline masters are generic, allowing you to adjust numbers to meet the individual needs of your students. As an added benefit, the pages may be used more than once, providing extra homework or classroom practice.

After each strategy study, students should record the facts that they have practiced and are committing to quick recall. The Addition Facts Table on page 18 is provided for this purpose. In addition to monitoring students' progress, the table reminds students that a large number of the facts can be found using very basic strategies and that few facts are really challenging to master.

Blank facts cards are provided on pages 48 through 51. Each card is marked with a facts strategy icon. As each new strategy and set of facts is introduced, students should add the corresponding cards to their collection. Students will enjoy making their own sets of cards for practice. Encourage students to make cards using the strategy that best helps them recall the facts. For example, although a student may be introduced to 9 + 3 in the Counting-on strategy, he or she may prefer to write the fact on a Make-a-Ten card because it "works better."

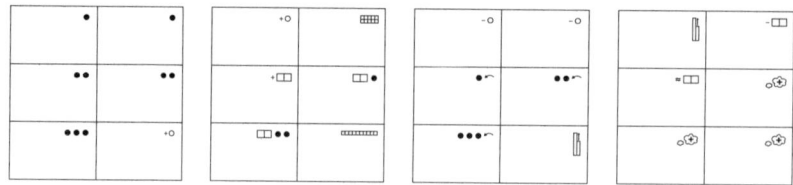

Review pages are included to help you and your students monitor progress. Students may wish to note the time required to complete each review on successive checks. Stress the importance of improving one's own time, rather than competing with classmates. Consider giving students different reviews, depending on their capabilities. Additional review pages for facts practice and skill maintenance are provided on pages 52 through 57. Selected solutions begin on page 58.

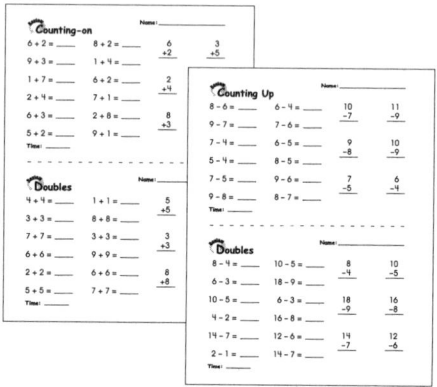

Addition facts are emphasized in this book, as they provide a foundation for subtraction facts. Strategies such as Counting Back are introduced to help students master the more challenging subtraction facts. Once students understand the nature of the relationship between addition and subtraction, they may simply identify the missing part to name a difference. Although addition and subtraction strategies are presented in different sections of this book, they need not be separated during instruction. For example, the Counting-on or Doubles strategies for addition could very naturally be combined with the Counting Back and Doubles strategies for subtraction.

Of special note: It is important that strategies come *from the students* whenever possible. Given the opportunity, students will naturally suggest ideas using shortcuts and patterns that help them think about each fact. Trust your students to identify an efficient way to approach each group of facts—their ideas may impress you! Always encourage each student to use a strategy that works best for him or her. This book is designed to highlight and expose children to different ways of thinking about facts, but the final decision on which strategies to use is the student's. Knowing that "their way" works for them builds students' confidence, and makes fact retention easier and more consistent.

Getting Started

Explain to students that they are going to learn their facts by using strategies. Tell them that a strategy is *a way of thinking* that helps them name a fact quickly and correctly.

Display a variety of facts, such as:

5 + 2   6 + 7   8 + 5   9 + 4   7 + 1   6 + 8   6 + 6   3 + 9   0 + 8

Have students pick any three facts to solve. After about 10-15 seconds, ask: *Which facts did you solve? How did you know the answer? Did anyone use the same strategy? A different strategy?* Explain that students will be thinking about their *thinking* as they master the basic facts.

Addition Facts Strategies

Counting-on and the Zero Property

Counting-on: This group of facts is the largest. Students will be encouraged to see how many facts they can learn using this easy strategy! The 43 Counting-on facts include:

1 + 1   2 + 1   3 + 1   4 + 1   5 + 1   6 + 1   7 + 1   8 + 1   9 + 1
1 + 2   1 + 3   1 + 4   1 + 5   1 + 6   1 + 7   1 + 8   1 + 9
2 + 2   3 + 2   4 + 2   5 + 2   6 + 2   7 + 2   8 + 2   9 + 2
2 + 4   2 + 5   2 + 6   2 + 7   2 + 8   2 + 9
4 + 3   5 + 3   6 + 3   7 + 3   8 + 3   9 + 3
3 + 4   3 + 5   3 + 6   3 + 7   3 + 8   3 + 9

The Zero Property: Some students may think that whenever they add, they must get a larger sum. They may need convincing that adding zero to a number does not change its value. This is called the *identity*, or *zero property* where (a + 0) = a = (0 + a). This can also be thought of as counting-on zero. This strategy can be modeled using blocks, counters, or a number line. Be sure to model using zero as either addend (5 + 0 and 0 + 5). The 19 Counting-on zero facts are:

0 + 0
0 + 1   0 + 2   0 + 3   0 + 4   0 + 5   0 + 6   0 + 7   0 + 8   0 + 9
1 + 0   2 + 0   3 + 0   4 + 0   5 + 0   6 + 0   7 + 0   8 + 0   9 + 0

Cupful Count-On (page 19): For younger students, counting-on without starting at one can present a challenge. To aid in developing this concept, model counting out and placing five counters into a paper cup. Write the numeral 5 on the cup. Drop in one more counter. Ask: *How many counters are in the cup? How did you know?* Students can point to the cup and say "five" and then to the extra counter and say "six." Repeat using a different number, such as seven, and drop in two counters. Students will suggest saying "seven" and then "eight, nine" to count the total. Activity page 19 can be customized for repeated use. Make one copy of the page and then write the numerals 1 through 9 on the cups. Duplicate that page for the class. The original activity page can be used for review and additional practice.

Hop Along, Harvey! (page 20): Copy the activity page. Write the numerals 0 through 9 on the lily pads, then duplicate it for use with the class. This number line model for addition is more abstract, so careful attention must be made to point out that counting begins at zero, not at one. Point out that the space, or hop, represents a given quantity. Have students place their fingers on a given lily pad number and then "hop" one, two, or three spaces, from lily pad to lily pad, towards the fly. For additional challenge, write the sums on a different copy, and have the students write the lily pad numbers.

Turn It Around (page 21): Use interlocking cubes to model the commutative property where 6 + 2 = 2 + 6. Make a two-colored stick showing six cubes of one color and two of a second. Explain that counting-on two from six instead of counting-on six from two is a shortcut. Show the sum is eight either way. Students may name a fact partner its "turnaround." Use additional examples and different manipulatives to reinforce the strategy counting-on from the larger addend.

Facts Table and the Counting-on and Zero Facts Cards

Distribute the addition facts table to each student, and discuss how it is organized. Explain that although they may know more facts than the Counting-on and Zero group, at this time they will write only the sums that they have explored so far. In this way, they will keep track of which facts they have studied and mastered, and watch their progress as they move through each new strategy.

+	0	1	2	3	4	5	6	7	8	9
0	0	1	2	3	4	5	6	7	8	9
1	1	2	3	4	5	6	7	8	9	10
2	2	3	4	5	6	7	8	9	10	11
3	3	4	5	6	7	8	9	10	11	12
4	4	5	6	7						
5	5	6	7	8						
6	6	7	8	9						
7	7	8	9	10						
8	8	9	10	11						
9	9	10	11	12						

Total Facts Completed: 64

Model filling in the table using a large addition table posted in the classroom. Write the zero sums along the horizontal (0+) and vertical (+0) axes. Next, record the Counting-on One, Two, Three, and Zero facts, noting the patterns and total number of facts completed (64). This is more than half the facts!

Introduce the fact cards on page 48. Remind students that the zero and dot icons can stand for counters to be added to a cup, or hops on the number line.

Doubles

Most students have little trouble learning the doubles. They are a very important group, as many other facts can be derived from them. Although there are ten facts in this group, students need only to learn six new facts as the other four overlap with the Counting-on group. Explain that for this reason, students should know these facts *twice* as well!

$0+0$ $1+1$ $2+2$ $3+3$ **$4+4$ $5+5$ $6+6$ $7+7$ $8+8$ $9+9$**

Dora's Dots (page 22): This activity requires some preparation, but the lasting impression it makes it is well worth the time. You will need nine pieces of construction paper, a paintbrush, and one color of tempera paint. Fold, then unfold, each piece of construction paper in half to make a crease down the center. Tell Dora's story, calling on a student to help when needed:

Dora was a little girl who just loved dots! She had a polka dot bedroom, a polka dot lunch box, a polka dot sweater, and even polka dot shoes! So, what do you think she painted whenever she had a chance? (polka dots!)

One rainy day, she decided to do just that. She got out her paints and painted one lovely dot. (Have a student paint a dot on one side of the construction paper.)

Now Dora had a little sister who was very mischievous. Mary was her name. Mary saw what Dora had painted, and when Dora wasn't looking, what do you think she did? She folded Dora's painting! (Have a volunteer fold the paper.) *Dora wasn't very happy at first, but when she unfolded her paper, a great big smile came across her face. Can you guess why?* (Have students predict.) *Now, instead of one dot, there were two!* (Have "Dora" unfold the paper to show this.)

Next, Dora painted two dots. What do you think Mary did? (She folded Dora's paper again.) (Have two additional volunteers act this out.) *What do you think happened when Dora opened it up? (There were four dots.)*

Continue with the story, having Dora paint three, four, and up to nine dots on one side of the paper, then having Mary fold each to make a double. You may wish to do up to five dots in one class session, then continue from six to nine dots during a following class period.

Display and organize all of the dot paintings. Have students describe what the dot pictures show using numbers and symbols. Write each doubles fact below each picture and have students look for patterns. Students will notice that the addends increase by one, and that the sums are all even numbers counting by twos.

1 + 1 = 2	2 + 2 = 4	3 + 3 = 6	4 + 4 = 8	5 + 5 = 10

Distribute copies of Dora's Dots (page 22) and have students draw each dot reflection and write a matching number sentence to complete the page.

Twice is Nice! (page 23): Students will enjoy practicing their Doubles as they play this game!

Facts Table and Doubles Facts Cards

Record the Doubles facts on the Facts Table, noting the diagonal pattern from the upper right corner to the lower left corner of the table. Students should count 70 completed squares.

Next, introduce the Doubles Facts Cards.

Review: Counting-on and Doubles (page 24)

+	0	1	2	3	4	5	6	7	8	9
0	0	1	2	3	4	5	6	7	8	9
1	1	2	3	4	5	6	7	8	9	10
2	2	3	4	5	6	7	8	9	10	11
3	3	4	5	6	7	8	9	10	11	12
4	4	5	6	7	8					
5	5	6	7	8		10				
6	6	7	8	9			12			
7	7	8	9	10				14		
8	8	9	10	11					16	
9	9	10	11	12						18

Total Facts Completed: 70

Complements of Ten

Special emphasis is placed on this section, as knowing addends of ten may be used to combine larger addends (Hidden Ten strategy). Ten is a benchmark in our number system: recognizing numbers that make a ten is vital in working with numbers of all sizes. Again, there is overlap with facts studied earlier, so only two new facts will be added to the table. These facts are:

1 + 9   2 + 8   3 + 7   **4 + 6**   5 + 5   **6 + 4**   7 + 3   8 + 2   9 + 1

Brenda's Blocks (page 25): This problem-solving activity introduces students to different ways of making ten. Give small groups of students a container filled with two colors of interlocking cubes. Ask a volunteer to take ten cubes from a container and describe the "bagful" he or she has taken. Working in small groups, have students take cubes from the container and record at least four different combinations for making ten. Ask groups to describe their "bags," one at a time. Ask: *Does anyone else have a bag that is the same?*

Have students represent the "bags" using interlocking cubes to make sticks that show each combination of ten. After the sticks are made, place them vertically on the chalk tray. Ask: *How can we record the set or fact? Who has a different fact?* Use the words, *part* and *total*, *addend* and *sum*, when describing the sticks. When writing number sentences, agree which color will be named first. For example, 6 blue + 4 yellow = 10.

Have students predict what additional combinations could be made. Ask: *Do we have all the combinations? How do you know? What other combinations could we make?* Students will likely suggest ordering the sticks in some way. Do so, having them describe how they are organizing the sticks and how this helps them know they have included all the ways to make ten. Continue naming ways to make ten until all nine ways are displayed. (In this case, zero is not included as an addend.) Have students describe what they see. They will likely describe staircases and will notice that when there is one more blue cube, there is one fewer yellow cube.

Show the 7 blue + 3 yellow stick and the 3 blue + 7 yellow stick. Ask: *How are these alike? How are these different?* Have students identify other pairs of sticks that demonstrate the commutative property, or turnaround facts. Ask: *Does 5 + 5 have a turnaround? Why not?*

String Beads (page 26): This is a manageable and easy-to-make manipulative that is perfect for kinesthetic learners. String ten same-color beads on a pipe cleaner. Secure the beads by making a loop at each end of the pipe cleaner. Have students "break" the set of beads in different ways and name the parts on each side. They can also flip the string beads to show each turnaround fact. For example:

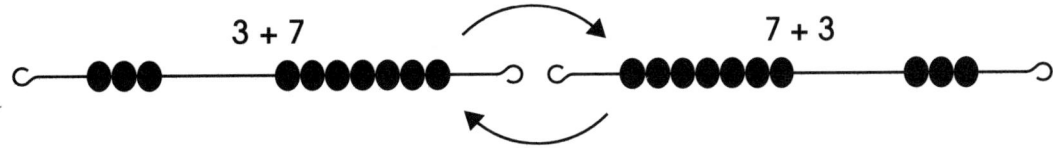

Ten-Frame Facts (page 27): The ten-frame is a powerful visual aid that can be used in numerous ways. Introduce the ten-frame using a transparency of page 27. Explain that quantities are shown by placing markers in the frame, beginning in the left-hand box in the top row. Place ten markers, one at a time, in the frame and count aloud with students from left to right, top to bottom:

❶	❷	❸	❹	❺
❻	❼	❽	❾	❿

Place four markers in the frame and flash it on the overhead projector for a second. Ask: *How many markers did you see?* Show the flashed ten-frame again and have students explain how they knew there were four markers.

Some will mention that they saw one less than five, two sets of two, or they "just knew it." Continue, using larger numbers up to ten.

Show six markers on the ten-frame. Ask: *How many filled spaces? How many are not filled?* Name the fact (6 + 4 = 10). Repeat, having students name pairs of numbers that make ten. Students can cut out the ten-frame fact cards on page 27, then work in small groups to practice naming complements of ten using these visual aids.

Totally Ten! (page 28): These puzzles illustrate the part-part-total relationship of facts. Model this idea using interlocking cubes. Begin by making a stick of ten green. Count aloud to show ten green. Use two yellows and eight reds to make a second stick of ten. Place the two sticks side by side. Ask: *How many in the yellow/red stick? How do you know? What two parts do you see? What is the total?* This part-part-total language and modeling fosters understanding of number family relationships. Have students do the page using cubes. Have students write a number sentence (or sentences) to match each puzzle.

Facts Table and Complements of Ten Cards
Record the sums to ten on the Facts Table, writing a 10 to show sums. Students will be excited to see a diagonal line of tens from the upper right to lower left corner of the square. It crisscrosses the doubles diagonal. So far, they should count 67 squares with sums.

Introduce the fact cards with the Ten-Frame icon and add the cards to each student's set.

+	0	1	2	3	4	5	6	7	8	9
0	0	1	2	3	4	5	6	7	8	9
1	1	2	3	4	5	6	7	8	9	10
2	2	3	4	5	6	7	8	9	10	11
3	3	4	5	6	7	8	9	10	11	12
4	4	5	6	7	8		10			
5	5	6	7	8		10				
6	6	7	8	9	10		12			
7	7	8	9	10				14		
8	8	9	10	11					16	
9	9	10	11	12						18

Total Facts Completed: 72

Doubles-Plus Facts

Doubles-Plus-One

The ten new facts in this group are:

   4 + 5   5 + 4   5 + 6   6 + 5   6 + 7   7 + 6   7 + 8   8 + 7   8 + 9   9 + 8

Display these facts and have pairs of students discuss the thinking they use to find each sum. Encourage students to share all the different ways.

One More Dot (page 29): Remind students of the Dora and Mary story. Have sticky dots on hand to act out part two of the story. Display the dot paintings and tell how Mary gets into more mischief:

Dora hung her doubles pictures on her bedroom wall. That evening, Mary found some dot stickers in Dora's craft box. She placed one at a time on each of Dora's paintings. (Have students place one sticky dot on each paper.) *When Dora saw what Mary had done, she described what she saw. What do you think she said?*

Have students discuss the paintings and record what they say with numbers. For example, they may see (4 + 4) +1 or 4 + (4 + 1). Help them understand this associative property of addition. They may rename what they see as 8 + 1 or 4 + 5 or 5 + 4. Students will notice that the sums are all odd numbers. Refer to the dot pictures and have them explain the reason for this. Have students complete page 29 to practice identifying Doubles-Plus-One facts.

Helping Double (page 30): This activity helps students identify and use a double to name sums.

Facts Table and the Doubles-Plus-One Cards
Locate and record the facts on the table. They will run alongside the doubles diagonal. Again, quite a bit of overlap will occur. Mention that this gives students options on strategies—they may use what works best for *them*!

Introduce the Doubles-Plus-One icon. Add the Doubles-Plus-One cards to each student's facts deck.

+	0	1	2	3	4	5	6	7	8	9
0	0	1	2	3	4	5	6	7	8	9
1	1	2	3	4	5	6	7	8	9	10
2	2	3	4	5	6	7	8	9	10	11
3	3	4	5	6	7	8	9	10	11	12
4	4	5	6	7	8	9	10			
5	5	6	7	8	9	10	11			
6	6	7	8	9	10	11	12	13		
7	7	8	9	10			13	14	15	
8	8	9	10	11				15	16	17
9	9	10	11	12					17	18

Total Facts Completed: 82

Doubles-Plus-Two

The six new facts in this group are:

   5 + 7   7 + 5   6 + 8   8 + 6   7 + 9   9 + 7

Display these facts and have pairs of students discuss the thinking they use to find each sum.

Doubles + 2 Connect (page 31): One way to think about this group of facts may be to double the smaller addend and count-on two more. Students may practice this thinking as they play the game on this page.

Give and Take (page 32): Use a balance to model this "give and take" thinking, similar to the description on the activity page. A second way to think about the Doubles-Plus Two facts might be described using compensation, where one addend "shares" with another. Use five yellow and five green interlocking cubes to make a two-colored stick of ten. Break the stick in half to show 5 + 5 = 10. Put the stick together and break it again, this time showing 4 + 6. Explain that this is why these facts are sometimes called "hidden doubles."

Have students describe the parts they see. Ask: *Can you still see the 5 + 5? What happened?* Students may say that one part "gave" one cube to the other side, making one part one cube less, and the other part one cube more. Repeat showing 6 + 6 and 5 + 7.

Facts Table and Doubles-Plus-Two Cards
Conduct a class discussion about the two strategies for this set of facts. Encourage the students to choose the strategy that helps them to recall the facts more quickly.

They will be delighted to see that sums of these facts will create yet another diagonal line outside the Doubles-Plus-One facts. The overlap area contains smaller addends (such as 3 + 1), and may be difficult to see.

+	0	1	2	3	4	5	6	7	8	9
0	0	1	2	3	4	5	6	7	8	9
1	1	2	3	4	5	6	7	8	9	10
2	2	3	4	5	6	7	8	9	10	11
3	3	4	5	6	7	8	9	10	11	12
4	4	5	6	7	8	9	10			
5	5	6	7	8	9	10	11	12		
6	6	7	8	9	10	11	12	13	14	
7	7	8	9	10		12	13	14	15	16
8	8	9	10	11			14	15	16	17
9	9	10	11	12				16	17	18

Add the Doubles-Plus-Two facts cards to each student's deck.

Total Facts Completed: 82

Review: Doubles and Doubles-Plus-One and Doubles-Plus-Two (Page 33)

Make-a-Ten

There are twelve new facts in this group:

```
7 + 4   4 + 7   8 + 4   4 + 8   8 + 5   5 + 8
9 + 4   4 + 9   9 + 5   5 + 9   9 + 6   6 + 9
```

Students will look forward to filling in the last "holes" on their addition table to show all 100 facts.

Where's the Ten? (page 34): Have students use a pipe cleaner and ten each of two different color beads to make a counter similar to the one described on page 9.

8 + 5 =

(8 + 2) + 3 = 10 + 3

Have students show 8 + 5 using their bead counter. Count and slide eight beads to the left of the counter. Then count out five more, joining them together with the eight beads. Ask: *How many in all? How did you know? Did anyone use a shortcut to count the beads?* Students will say that they saw ten of one color and three more of the second color. Explain that they made a ten when they added 8 + 5 by making 8 + 2 in one color, and then added three more of the second color, or (8 + 2) + 3 = 13. Repeat this strategy with additional examples, such as 7 + 6 and 9 + 5. Students will need to think about the Make-a-Ten strategy to make sense of this model.

Pondering Plus 9 (page 35): Although all of the Plus 9 facts can be named using other strategies described thus far, students may find that the Plus 9 Pattern is useful as well. Have students be fact "detectives" and work in small groups to compose a rule that can be used to name a sum of a Plus 9 fact.

Review: Make-a-Ten and Mixed Addition Facts (page 36)

Adding Machines Review (page 37): This activity page can be customized for repeated use. Make one copy of the activity page and write eight numbers on the left side of each adding machine. Duplicate that page. Students will name the sums for each column. For a challenge, duplicate a page with the sums written in. Students have to name the addends.

Facts Table and Make-a-Ten Facts Cards
The Facts Table is finally complete with a total of 100 facts! Add the Make-A-Ten facts cards to each student's deck.

+	0	1	2	3	4	5	6	7	8	9
0	0	1	2	3	4	5	6	7	8	9
1	1	2	3	4	5	6	7	8	9	10
2	2	3	4	5	6	7	8	9	10	11
3	3	4	5	6	7	8	9	10	11	12
4	4	5	6	7	8	9	10	**11**	**12**	**13**
5	5	6	7	8	9	10	11	12	13	**14**
6	6	7	8	9	10	11	12	13	14	**15**
7	7	8	9	10	**11**	12	13	14	15	16
8	8	9	10	11	**12**	13	14	15	16	17
9	9	10	11	12	**13**	**14**	**15**	16	17	18

Total Facts Completed: 100!

Subtraction Facts Strategies

Counting Back One, Two, or Three

This group of 27 facts is the largest and includes:

2 – 1	3 – 1	4 – 1	5 – 1	6 – 1	7 – 1	8 – 1	9 – 1	10 – 1		
3 – 2	4 – 2	5 – 2	6 – 2	7 – 2	8 – 2	9 – 2	10 – 2	11 – 2		
4 – 3	5 – 3	6 – 3	7 – 3		8 – 3		9 – 3	10 – 3	11 – 3	12 – 3

This strategy can be easily illustrated with take-away story problems where students can physically remove objects from a set. For an interesting discussion, ask: *Do these subtraction facts have turnaround partners?*

There's a Hole in My Bucket (page 38): This activity can be customized for repeated use. Make one copy of the page and write the numbers 1 through 9 on the buckets. Duplicate that page for your class. Explain that each bucket is supposed to contain the number of rocks shown on each bucket, but some have fallen out. Have students find the remaining number of rocks in each bucket by counting back one, two, or three from the number shown on each bucket. Students then write the subtraction fact.

Zero Property

List examples of the 19 zero facts and have students describe how they find or know the answers.

0 – 0 1 – 0 2 – 0 3 – 0 4 – 0 5 – 0 6 – 0 7 – 0 8 – 0 9 – 0
       1 – 1 2 – 2 3 – 3 4 – 4 5 – 5 6 – 6 7 – 7 8 – 8 9 – 9

Children may suggest making two groups: those facts having an answer of 0, and those that don't. Ask: *What do the facts in each group have in common? How does this help you know the answer quickly?*

All or Nothing (page 39): Model this game by playing it with the class, then have pairs of students play additional rounds.

Review: Counting Back and the Zero Property (page 40)

Counting Up

Note that these 17 facts have a difference of 1, 2, or 3 between the minuend and subtrahend. The values of the two numbers are close. This is why it is convenient to count up to find the difference.

5 − 4	6 − 4	7 − 4		6 − 5	7 − 5	8 − 5		7 − 6	8 − 6	9 − 6
8 − 7	9 − 7	10 − 7		9 − 8	10 − 8	11 − 8		10 − 9	11 − 9	

Demonstrate this strategy using interlocking cubes or a number line. Explain that subtraction can show the difference between two numbers. Tell a story problem such as, *Diane's worm is seven (units) long and Michael's is five (units) long. How much longer is Diane's worm than Michael's?* The language in this problem may be particularly difficult. Therefore, it is important for students to use objects to act out the problem. Ask: *What is the **difference** between seven (units) and five (units)?* Students will suggest comparing both numbers (of cubes or on the number line) and counting up two (units) to find the difference.

Counting Up can also be illustrated using counters with a story problem. In this case, keeping the one-to-one correspondence may be more challenging for students. Students may also want to use the Counting Up strategy to make change.

What's the Difference? (page 41): Give students practice using this strategy by having them complete this page.

Doubles

The five subtraction doubles facts come easily for students familiar with the addition doubles:

8 − 4   10 − 5   12 − 6   14 − 7   16 − 8

Drops on Doubles (page 42): Students will enjoy practicing their doubles as they complete this page.

Review: Counting Up and Doubles (page 43)

Near Doubles

This group of ten facts will pose a challenge to many students. With subtraction, near doubles are not identified as easily as in the case of addition.

9 – 4   9 – 5   11 – 5   11 – 6   13 – 6   13 – 7   15 – 7   15 – 8   17 – 8   17 – 9

Helping Doubles II (page 44): Have students work together in pairs or small groups and talk about their thinking. Share strategies as a whole class.

Use Addition

These 20 facts use the number family relationships to name subtraction facts.

10-4   10-6   13-4   13-9   15-6   15-9   11-4   11-7   13-5   13-8   16-7
16-9   12-4   12-8   14-5   14-9   12-5   12-7   14-6   14-8

This strategy may be used with *all* of the subtraction facts, and students may choose to rely more on this strategy to name subtraction facts, rather than the strategies described previously.

Missing Part Puzzles (page 45): These puzzles show the part-part-total and number family concepts of addition. Some students may need to use interlocking cubes to find the facts.

Review: Near Doubles and Use Addition (page 46)

Subtraction Review: All Facts (page 47)

Cumulative Review: Addition and Subtraction (pages 52 and 53)

Mixed Review: (page 54)

Turnaround Facts Review: (page 55)

Oral Facts Review: Addition and Subtraction (pages 56 and 57)

Using the Facts Cards

Blank facts cards for addition can be found on pages 48-49. The blank cards for subtraction facts can be found on pages 50-51. The facts cards are marked with strategy icons to aid students in quick recall of facts using the strategies. The number of cards required for each strategy group is shown.

If possible, laminate the cards or copy them on heavyweight paper to make them more durable. Use the cards to play facts games, such as *War*, in which the student having the higher (or lower) sum or difference claims both cards. *Concentration* is another game that can be played using the addition cards, where turnaround facts are matched. Invite students to create their own facts games and share them with classmates.

Addition Strategies

Counting-on 1 ● 17 cards

Counting-on 2 ● ● 14 cards

Counting-on 3 ● ● ● 12 cards

Zero Property +○ 19 cards

Doubles + ☐☐ 6 cards

Complements of Ten ▦ 2 cards

Doubles-Plus 1 ☐☐ ● 10 cards

Doubles-Plus 2 ☐☐ ● ● 6 cards

Make-a-Ten ▭▭▭▭▭ 12 cards

Subtraction Strategies

Counting Back 1 ● ⌒ 9 cards

Counting Back 2 ● ● ⌒ 9 cards

Counting Back 3 ● ● ● ⌒ 9 cards

Zero Property −○ 19 cards

Counting Up 🁢 18 cards

Doubles − ☐☐ 5 cards

Near Doubles ≈ ☐☐ 10 cards

Use Addition ✿+ 20 cards

Addition Facts Table

Strategies

- ☐ **Counting-On**
- ☐ **Zero Property**
- ☐ **Doubles**
- ☐ **Complements of Ten**
- ☐ **Doubles Plus**
- ☐ **Make-a-Ten**

+	0	1	2	3	4	5	6	7	8	9
0										
1										
2										
3										
4										
5										
6										
7										
8										
9										

Name: _____

Cupful Count-On

+ Counting-on

The number on each cup shows how many counters are inside. How many altogether? Count on to decide. Write the fact.

[6] •• = __8__

6 + 2 = 8

Hop Along, Harvey!

Name: _____

+ Counting-on

Harvey is sitting on a lily pad. The ⤴ shows how many hops he takes towards the fly. Write the lily pad number where he lands.

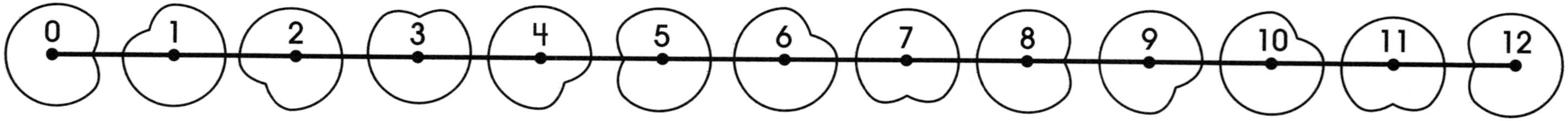

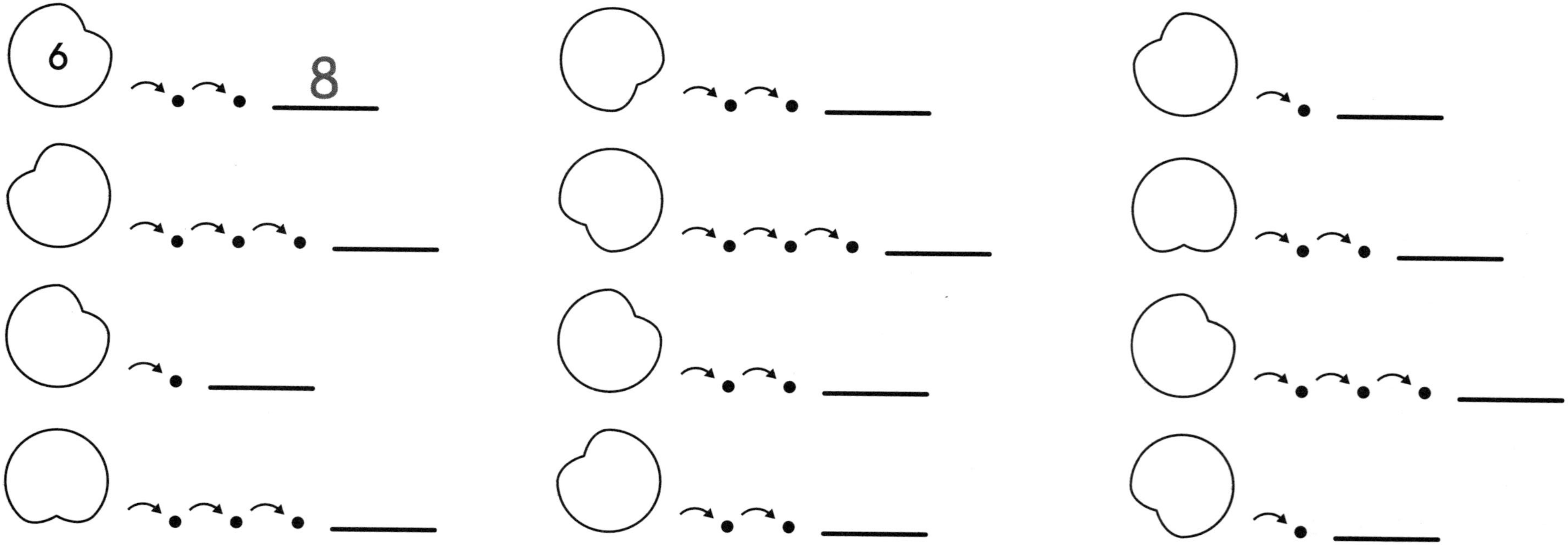

_8_

_6_

Turn It Around

Name: _____

+ Counting-on

Counting-on can help you know 6 + 3 and its turnaround fact, 3 + 6.
Just count on from the larger addend.

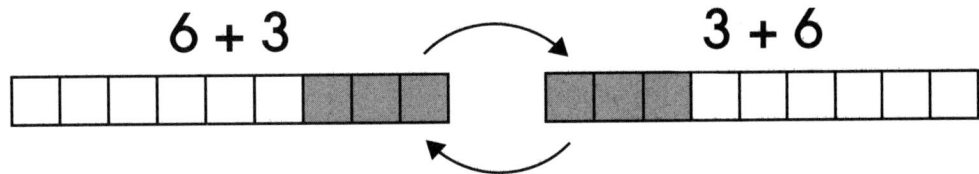

Circle the larger addend, then count on.
You may draw dots to help you count on.
Write the sums.

Think 6...7, 8, 9

⑥ · 7, 8

⑥ + 2̈ = ____   2 + 9 = ____

∴3 + ⑦ = ____   5 + 3 = ____

4 + 2 = ____   1 + 8 = ____

3 + 8 = ____   9 + 3 = ____

6 + 1 = ____   2 + 7 = ____

5 + 2 = ____   6 + 3 = ____

Dora's Dots

Name: _____

+ Doubles

What happens when Mary folds each dot picture?
Draw and write the doubles facts she makes.

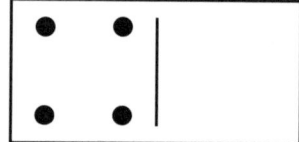 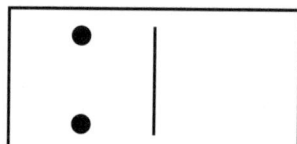 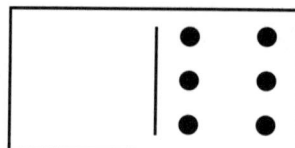

_____ _____ _____

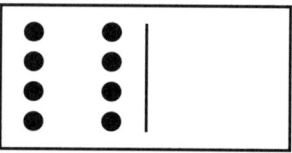 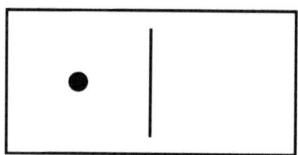 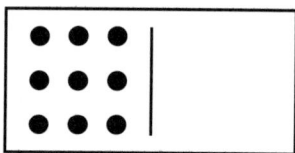

_____ _____ _____

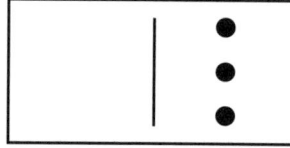 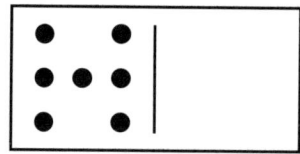 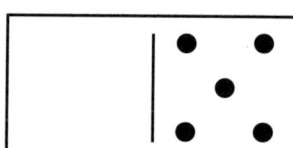

_____ _____ _____

Add the Doubles.

1	2	3	4	5	6	7	8	9
+1	+2	+3	+4	+5	+6	+7	+8	+9

What pattern do you see? _____

_____

Twice as Nice!

+ Doubles

You will need:
- a partner
- counters, one color for each player
- a paperclip to make a spinner

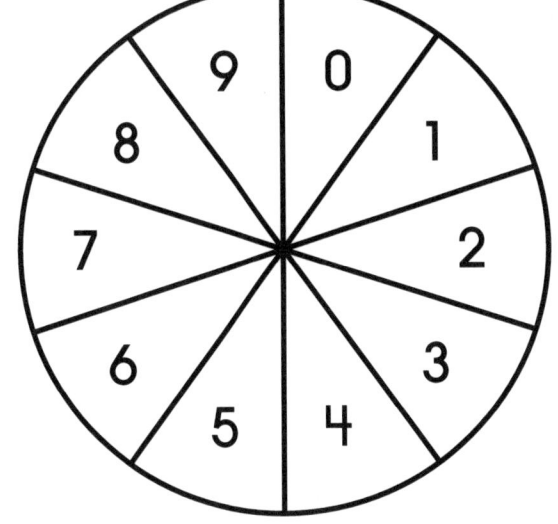

Directions:
Spin to decide who goes first.
Spin the spinner.
Double the number that you spin.
Put a counter on the sum.

The first player to have three in a row wins the game.

10	6	12	16	14
12	8	0	10	8
4	2	16	6	2
18	14	16	4	12
6	14	18	0	8

Review: Counting-on

Name: _____

6 + 2 = ____	8 + 2 = ____	6 +2 ___	3 +5 ___
9 + 3 = ____	1 + 4 = ____		
1 + 7 = ____	6 + 2 = ____	2 +4 ___	1 +6 ___
2 + 4 = ____	7 + 1 = ____		
6 + 3 = ____	2 + 8 = ____	8 +3 ___	7 +2 ___
5 + 2 = ____	9 + 1 = ____		

Time: _____

- -

Review: Doubles

Name: _____

4 + 4 = ____	1 + 1 = ____	5 +5 ___	9 +9 ___
3 + 3 = ____	8 + 8 = ____		
7 + 7 = ____	3 + 3 = ____	3 +3 ___	7 +7 ___
6 + 6 = ____	9 + 9 = ____		
2 + 2 = ____	6 + 6 = ____	8 +8 ___	2 +2 ___
5 + 5 = ____	7 + 7 = ____		

Time: _____

Brenda's Blocks

+ Complements of Ten

Brenda has a bag of 10 yellow and blue blocks.
What could her collection look like?
Draw 4 different groups of 10 blocks.
Write a number sentence for the blocks in each bag.

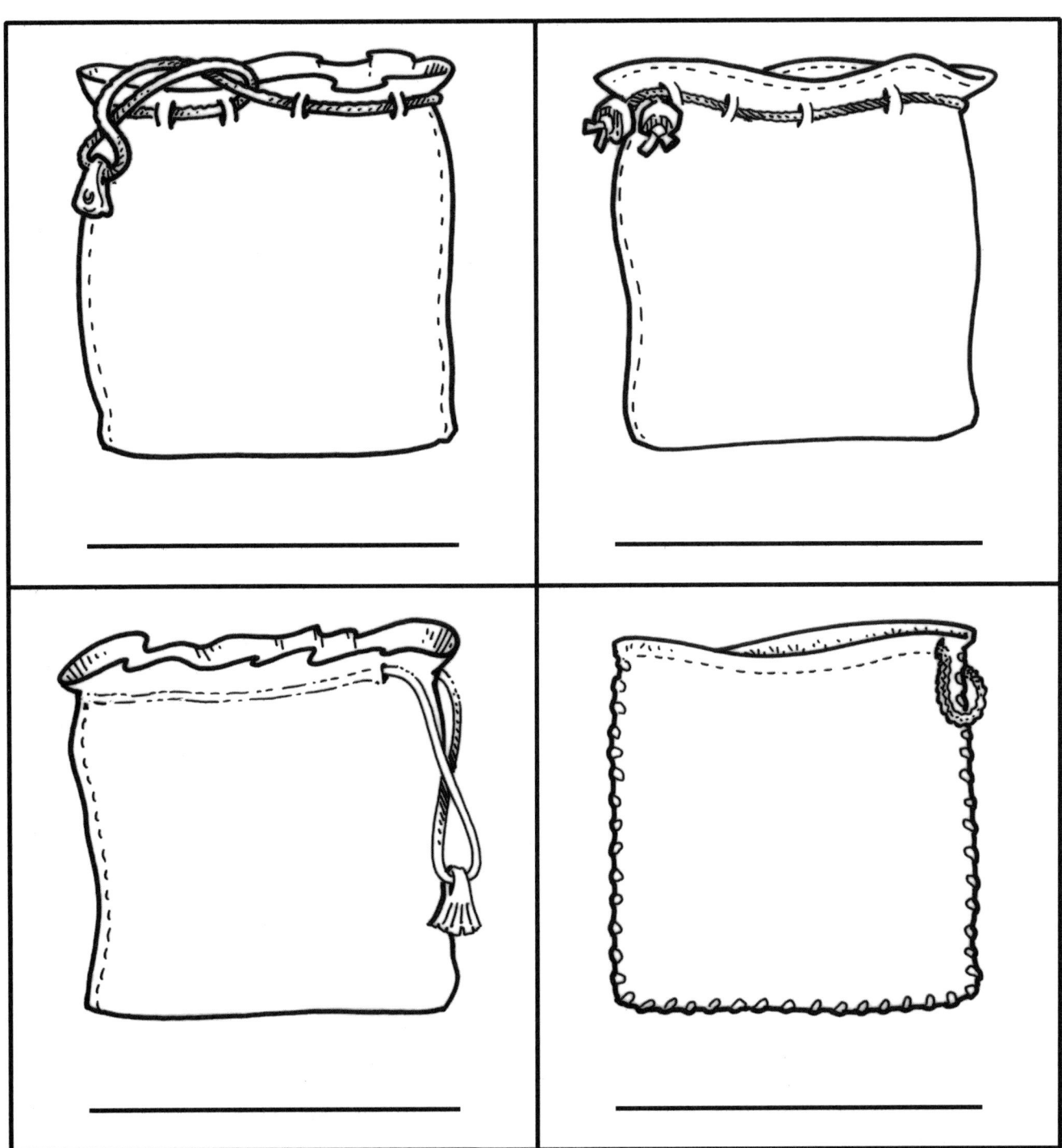

String Bead Sums

Name: _____

+ Complements of Ten

Sammy has string beads just like you. But some of his fell off!
Draw the beads to show 10 altogether.
Write the fact.

Draw a line to connect each turnaround fact.

Ten-Frame Facts

Name: _____

+ Complements of Ten

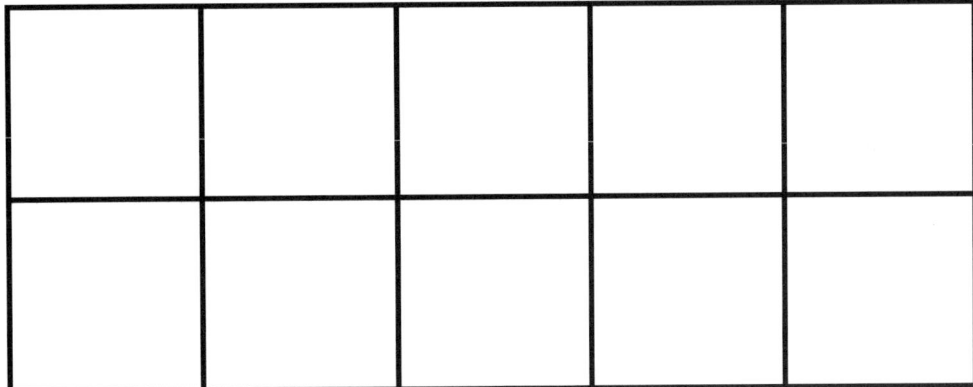

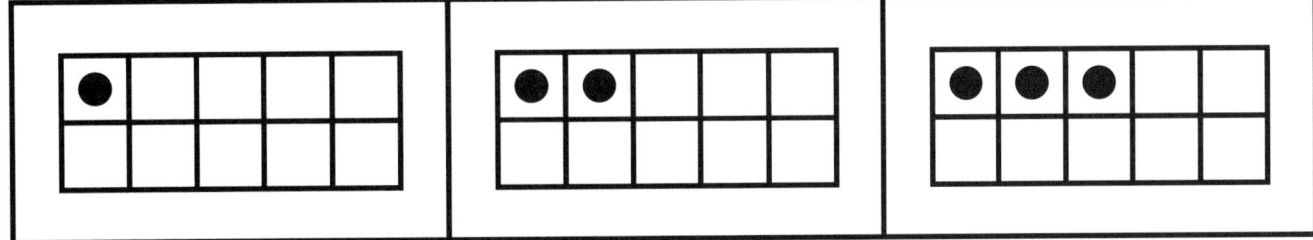

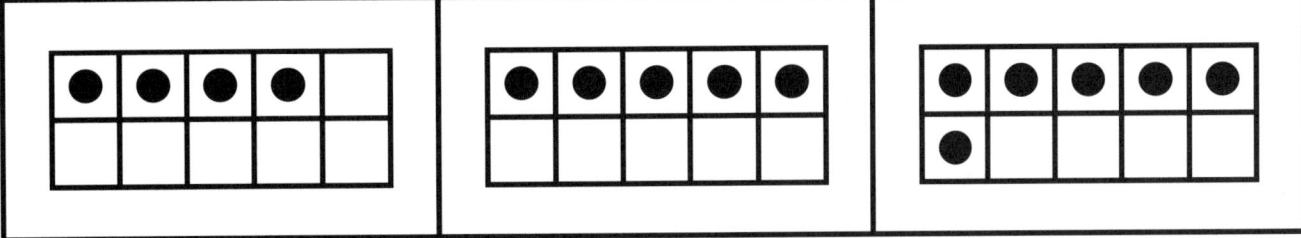

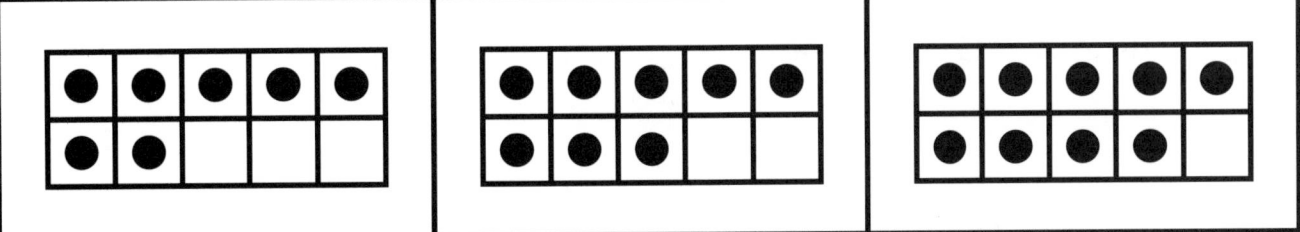

Totally Ten!

Name: _____

+ Complements of Ten

Name the parts of the tens bars.

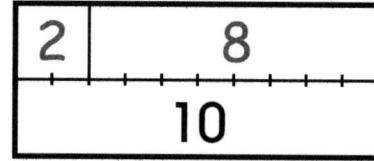 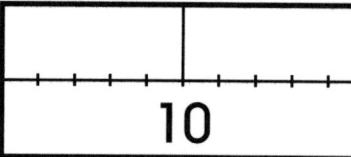 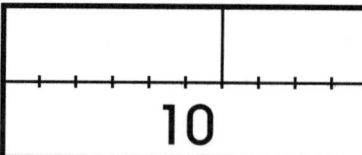

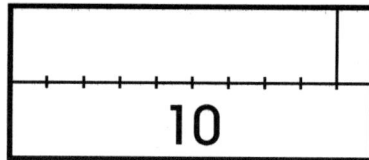 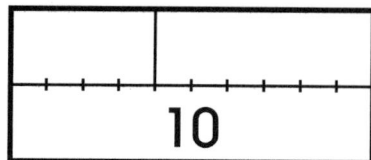 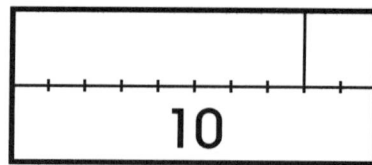

Name the missing part.
The tens bars can help you.

____ + 6 = 10   7 + ____ = 10

4 + ____ = 10   8 + ____ = 10

3 + ____ = 10   1 + ____ = 10

____ + 2 = 10   5 + ____ = 10

9 + ____ = 10

Match to make ten!

1 •   • 1
3 •   • 8
7 •   • 2
8 •   • 6
6 •   • 7
4 •   • 5
2 •   • 4
5 •   • 9
9 •   • 3

28   Facts in a Flash: Addition & Subtraction, Grades 1–3 • ID7140   © Ideal School Supply • A Division of Instructional Fair Group, Inc.

One More Dot!

Name: _____

+ Doubles Plus

Help Mary put a sticky dot on Dora's Doubles pictures.
Draw a dot on each picture.
Write the Doubles + 1 fact that you made.

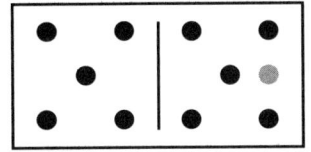  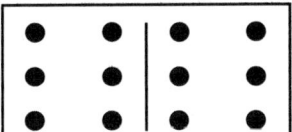

5 + 6 = 11 _____ _____

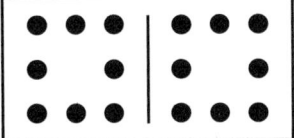 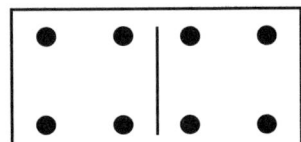 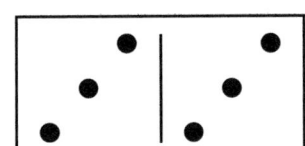

_____ _____ _____

Doubles + 1 Dot to Dot

7 →Double→ 14 →Plus 1→ 15

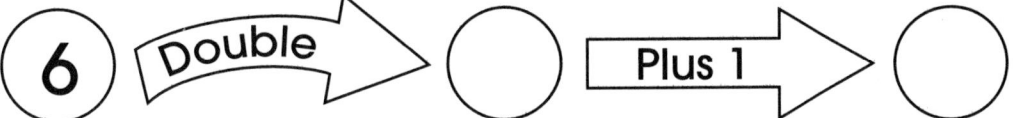
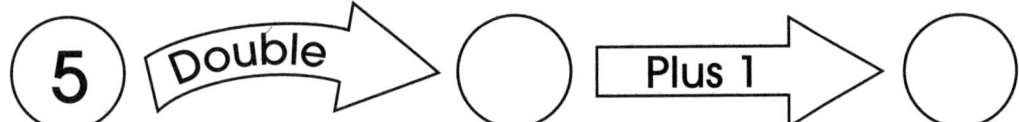
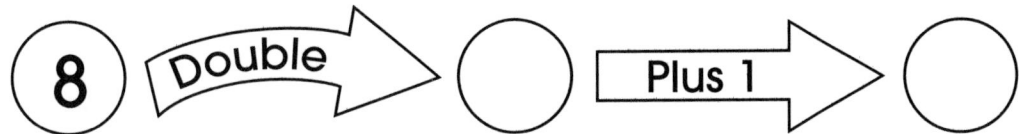

29

Helping Double

Name: _____

+ Doubles-Plus

For each fact, write the helping double.
Then add 1 more to name each sum.

Fact	Helping Double	+ 1	Sum
5 + 6	5 + 5	+ 1	11
3 + 4			
8 + 7			
7 + 6			
4 + 3			
8 + 9			
4 + 5			
6 + 7			
6 + 5			
9 + 8			
5 + 4			

Doubles + 2 Connect

Name: _____

+ Doubles-Plus

You will need:
- a partner
- counters
- a number cube labeled: 2, 3, 4, 5, 6, 7

Directions:
Take turns rolling the die.
Double the number rolled, then add 2.
Mark any ◯ that names the sum.
The first player to connect a path from top to bottom wins.

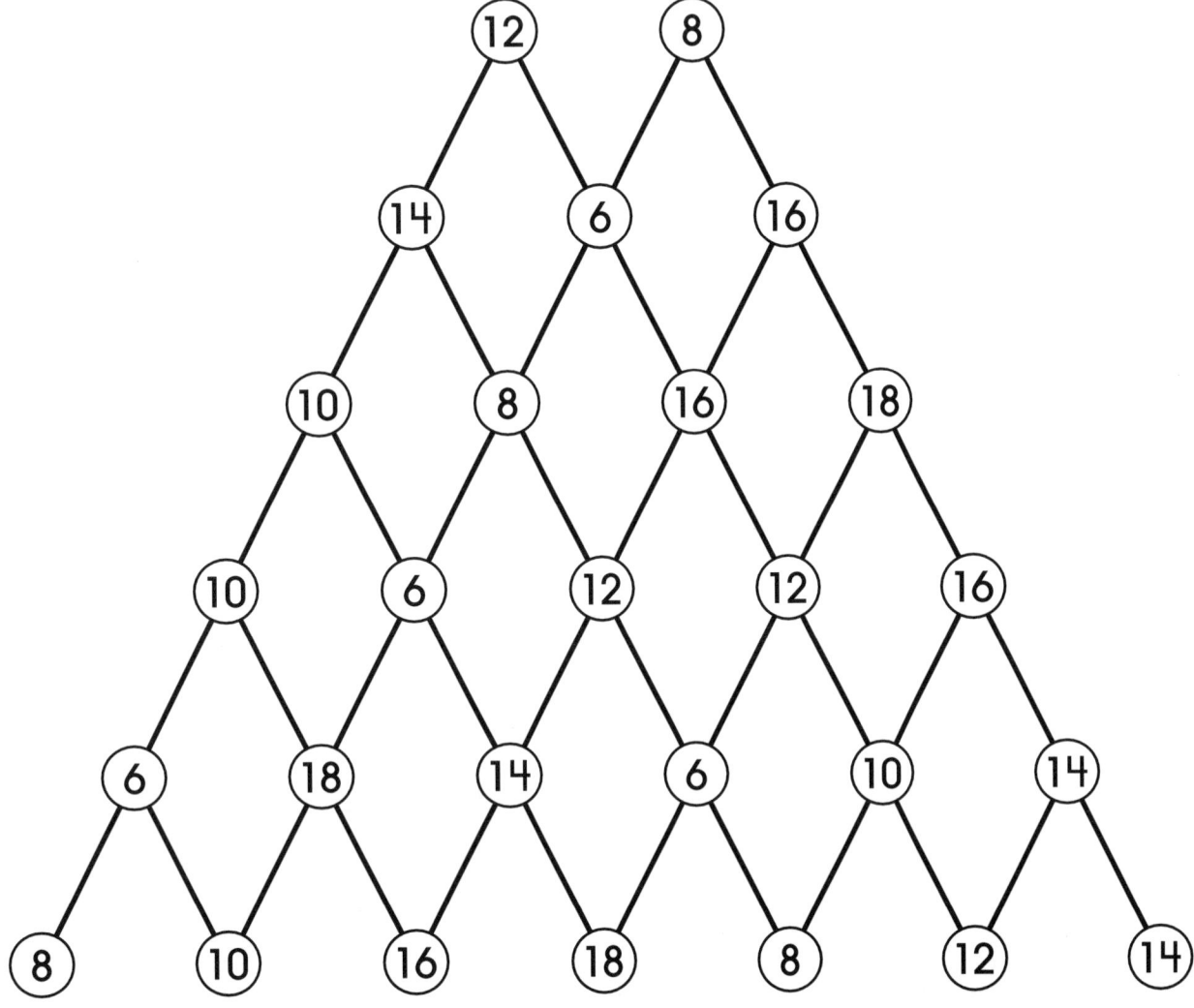

© Ideal School Supply • A Division of Instructional Fair Group, Inc.

Facts in a Flash: Addition & Subtraction, Grades 1-3 • ID7140

Give and Take

Name: _____

+ Doubles-Plus

This balance shows 6 + 4.  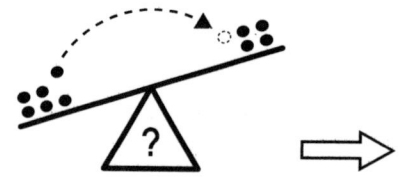 Give...and take! 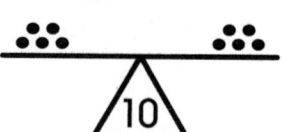 Now it shows 5 + 5.

Balance each scale to make a double. Write the sum in the △.

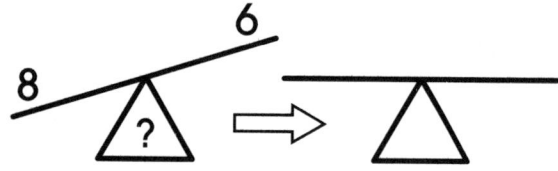 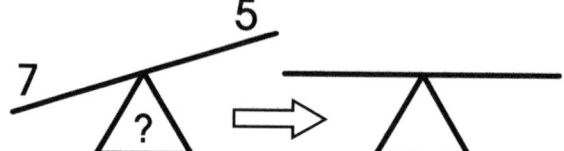

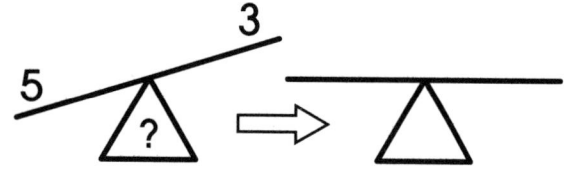 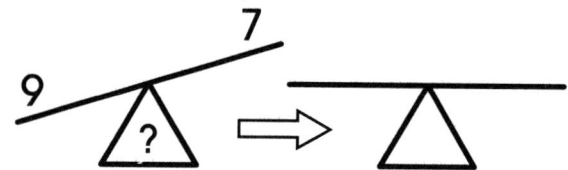

Find each Hidden Double and write the sum.

Fact	Hidden Double	Sum
8 + 6	7 + 7	14
6 + 4		
5 + 7		
9 + 7		
6 + 8		
7 + 5		

Name: _____

Review Doubles-Plus-One

4 + 5 = ____   7 + 6 = ____   6   7
                                  +5   +6
                                  ___   ___

6 + 7 = ____   9 + 8 = ____

3 + 2 = ____   3 + 4 = ____   9   5
                                  +8   +6
                                  ___   ___

4 + 3 = ____   7 + 8 = ____

8 + 9 = ____   5 + 6 = ____   7   4
                                  +8   +5
                                  ___   ___

5 + 4 = ____   8 + 7 = ____

Time: _____

- -

Name: _____

Review Doubles-Plus-Two

5 + 7 = ____   6 + 4 = ____   9   5
                                  +7   +7
                                  ___   ___

6 + 8 = ____   7 + 5 = ____

7 + 9 = ____   3 + 5 = ____   8   7
                                  +6   +9
                                  ___   ___

8 + 6 = ____   5 + 7 = ____

4 + 6 = ____   6 + 8 = ____   7   6
                                  +5   +8
                                  ___   ___

9 + 7 = ____   7 + 9 = ____

Time: _____

© Ideal School Supply • A Division of Instructional Fair Group, Inc.   Facts in a Flash: Addition & Subtraction, Grades 1–3 • ID7140

Where's the Ten?

Name: _____

+ Make-a-Ten

Where is the 10 hiding in each fact?
Write the numbers you think of to name each sum.

8 + 5 ___8 and 2 is 10. 3 more is 13.___
OR
___I know 5 + 5 is 10. 3 more is 13.___

7 + 4 _____

4 + 8 _____

9 + 5 _____

4 + 7 _____

8 + 4 _____

6 + 9 _____

4 + 9 _____

Name: _____

Pondering Plus 9

+ Make-a-Ten

Look for a pattern in the + 9 facts.

$$9 + 4 = 13 \qquad 9 + 5 = 14 \qquad 9 + 6 = 15$$
$$4 + 9 = 13 \qquad 5 + 9 = 14 \qquad 6 + 9 = 15$$

Describe the pattern you see in the addends and the sum.

_____

_____

Use the pattern to help you write the missing addend or sum.

9 + 5 = _____   7 + 9 = _____

_____ + 9 = 13   9 + _____ = 17

9 + _____ = 16   _____ + 9 = 15

_____ + 9 = 15   9 + 4 = _____

8 + 9 = _____   9 + _____ = 14

Make-a-Ten

Name: _____

7 + 4 = ____   5 + 8 = ____   6   4
                                    +9   +8
                                    ___   ___

9 + 4 = ____   9 + 6 = ____

4 + 8 = ____   5 + 9 = ____   5   9
                                    +8   +4
                                    ___   ___

9 + 5 = ____   8 + 4 = ____

8 + 5 = ____   4 + 9 = ____   9   7
                                    +5   +4
                                    ___   ___

6 + 9 = ____   4 + 7 = ____

Time: _____

- -

Mixed Addition Facts

Name: _____

4 + 4 = ____   2 + 9 = ____   5   8
                                    +7   +6
                                    ___   ___

6 + 3 = ____   6 + 6 = ____

7 + 5 = ____   5 + 3 = ____   9   8
                                    +4   +8
                                    ___   ___

1 + 9 = ____   7 + 6 = ____

8 + 7 = ____   8 + 9 = ____   7   5
                                    +4   +2
                                    ___   ___

6 + 5 = ____   9 + 6 = ____

Time: _____

Adding Machines

Name: _____

+ Review: All Facts Strategies

Each machine changes a number. Use fact strategies to help you name the numbers.

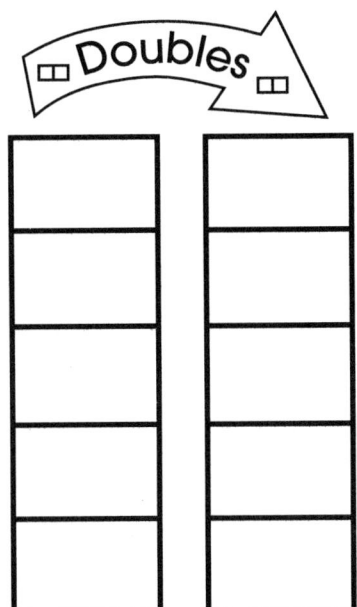

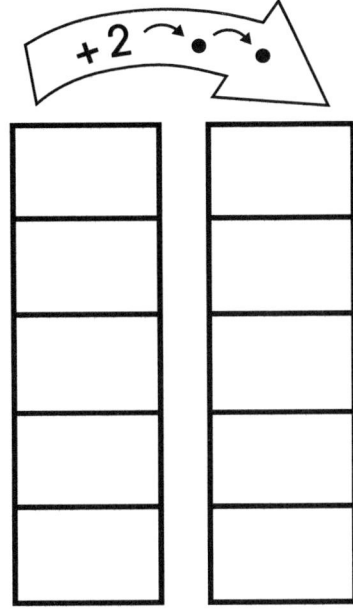

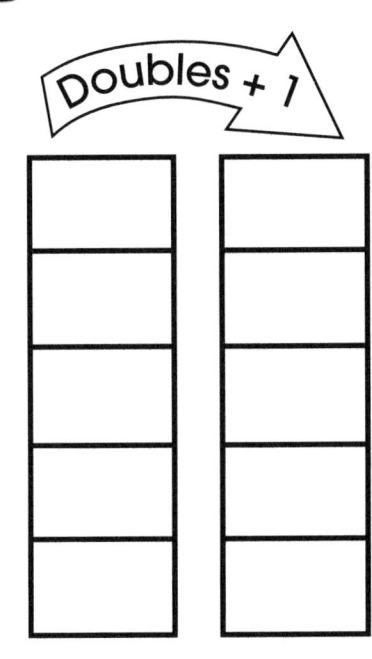

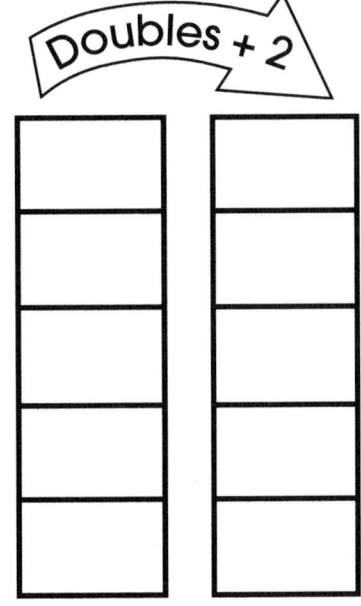

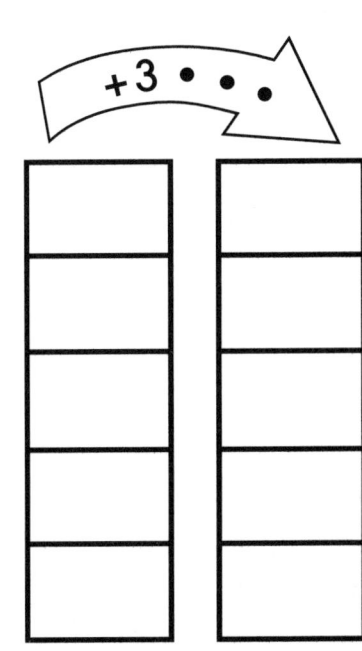

There's a Hole in My Bucket!

- Counting Back

Count back to name how many rocks are in each bucket.
Write the Counting Back fact.

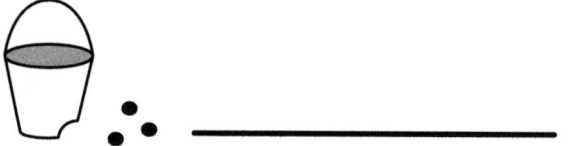 

All or Nothing

— Subtracting with Zero

You will need:
- a partner
- a paperclip to make a spinner

Directions:
Take turns.
Spin the spinner to decide if you take away all or nothing from each number.
Write a fact for your spin.
Keep playing until all 8 facts are filled.
Add the 8 differences.
The player with the smaller total is the winner.

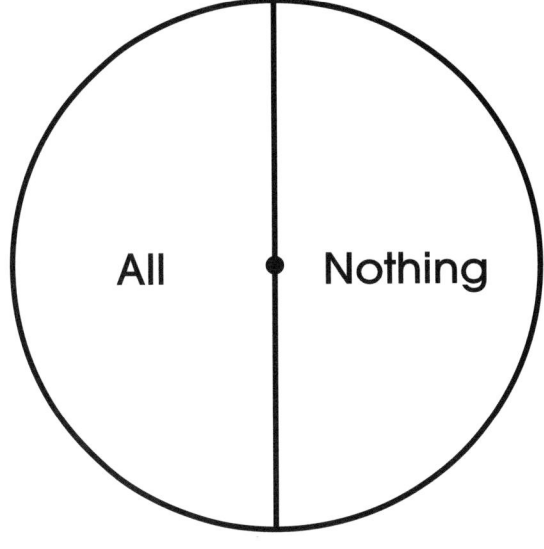

Player 1	Player 2
6	6
5	5
8	8
4	4
1	1
3	3
2	2
7	7
TOTAL:	TOTAL:

Counting Back

Name: _____

6 − 2 = ___   9 − 3 = ___   8   7
                                     −2   −1
                                     ___   ___

7 − 3 = ___   6 − 2 = ___

8 − 1 = ___   5 − 4 = ___   6   5
                                     −1   −3
                                     ___   ___

3 − 1 = ___   7 − 2 = ___

5 − 2 = ___   9 − 2 = ___   4   2
                                     −2   −1
                                     ___   ___

6 − 3 = ___   8 − 3 = ___

Time: _____

- -

Zero Property

Name: _____

5 − 5 = ___   2 − 0 = ___   9   8
                                     −9   −0
                                     ___   ___

6 − 0 = ___   1 − 1 = ___

3 − 3 = ___   4 − 4 = ___   6   5
                                     −6   −0
                                     ___   ___

5 − 0 = ___   7 − 0 = ___

4 − 0 = ___   8 − 8 = ___   3   2
                                     −0   −2
                                     ___   ___

7 − 7 = ___   9 − 0 = ___

Time: _____

What's the Difference?

Name: _____

- Counting Up

We can use subtraction to show the difference between two numbers.
Sam's tower is 8 cubes tall. Leah's tower is 6 cubes tall.
How much taller is Sam's tower than Leah's?

Think: How many more cubes?

8 − 6 = ?

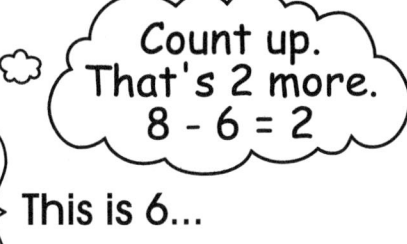

Count up. That's 2 more.
8 − 6 = 2

This is 6...

Write a subtraction fact to compare the tower pairs.
Count up to write your answer.

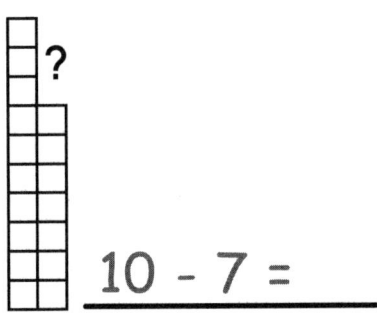

10 − 7 =

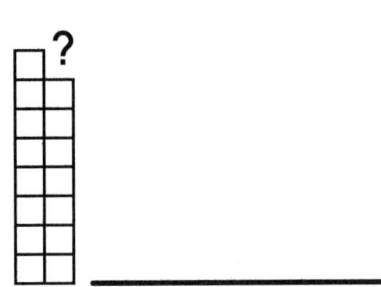

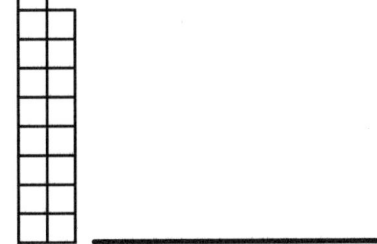

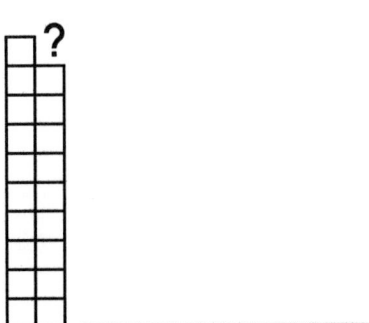

Drops on Doubles

Name: _____

- Doubles

Oops! As Ray was painting the clubhouse, he spilled white paint on his Doubles homework. Help Ray finish his homework.
Write the numbers over the "paint" to complete each number sentence.

◯ − 4 = 4   ◯ − 7 = 7

◯ − 8 = 8   ◯ − 3 = 3   ◯ − 9 = 9

◯ − 6 = 6   ◯ − 5 = 5   ◯ − 1 = 1

12 − 6 = 6   10 − ◯

8 − ◯   18 − ◯

4   16   6   14
− 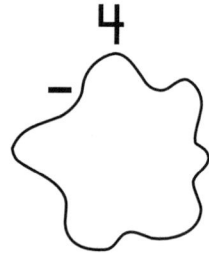   − 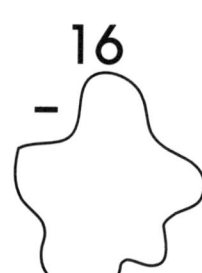   − 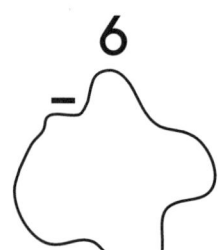   −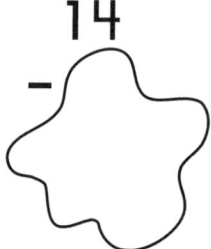

Counting Up

Name: _____

8 − 6 = ___　　6 − 4 = ___

```
  10        11
 − 7       − 9
 ___       ___
```

9 − 7 = ___　　7 − 6 = ___

7 − 4 = ___　　6 − 5 = ___

```
   9        10
 − 8       − 9
 ___       ___
```

5 − 4 = ___　　8 − 5 = ___

7 − 5 = ___　　9 − 6 = ___

```
   7         6
 − 5       − 4
 ___       ___
```

9 − 8 = ___　　8 − 7 = ___

Time: _____

- -

Doubles

Name: _____

8 − 4 = ___　　10 − 5 = ___

```
   8        10
 − 4       − 5
 ___       ___
```

6 − 3 = ___　　18 − 9 = ___

10 − 5 = ___　　6 − 3 = ___

```
  18        16
 − 9       − 8
 ___       ___
```

4 − 2 = ___　　16 − 8 = ___

14 − 7 = ___　　12 − 6 = ___

```
  14        12
 − 7       − 6
 ___       ___
```

2 − 1 = ___　　14 − 7 = ___

Time: _____

Helping Doubles II

Name: _____

- Near Doubles

Match each Near Double with a Double that helps you name it.

15 – 7   8 – 4

11 – 5   10 – 5

9 – 4   12 – 6

17 – 9   14 – 7

17 – 8   16 – 8

13 – 6   18 – 9

Tell a classmate how a Double can help you!

How do you know each difference?
Write about your thinking.

11 – 6 __12 – 6 is 6, 11 is one less, so it's 5. Check: 5 + 6 = 11__

9 – 5 _____

13 – 7 _____

17 – 9 _____

Missing Part Puzzles

Name: _____

- Use Addition

Write the missing part.
Write each addition fact and the subtraction fact for each box.

5	6
11	

5 + 6 = 11
11 − 5 = 6

	2
8	

_____
_____

9	
15	

_____
_____

5	
14	

_____
_____

7	
12	

_____
_____

	7
16	

_____
_____

5	
13	

_____
_____

7	
11	

_____
_____

	8
14	

_____
_____

Make your own.

_____
_____

_____
_____

_____
_____

45

Review: Near Doubles

Name: _____

9 - 4 = ___   9 - 5 = ___   17   11
                                         -8   -6
                                         ___   ___

11 - 5 = ___   15 - 8 = ___

17 - 8 = ___   11 - 6 = ___   15   13
                                         -8   -6
                                         ___   ___

13 - 6 = ___   13 - 7 = ___

15 - 7 = ___   11 - 5 = ___   13   9
                                         -7   -5
                                         ___   ___

17 - 9 = ___   9 - 4 = ___

Time: _____

- -

Review: Use Addition

Name: _____

12 - 8 = ___   11 - 7 = ___   13   15
                                         -4   -9
                                         ___   ___

14 - 5 = ___   13 - 8 = ___

12 - 4 = ___   16 - 9 = ___   10   14
                                         -6   -6
                                         ___   ___

14 - 9 = ___   16 - 7 = ___

13 - 5 = ___   13 - 9 = ___   10   12
                                         -4   -7
                                         ___   ___

11 - 4 = ___   15 - 6 = ___

Time: _____

Subtraction Facts

Name: _____

Match 3 facts that have the same difference.

```
   Subtract          Match
         \    A    /
```

8 - 2	9 - 2	11 - 7
9 - 5	13 - 9	15 - 9
6 - 1	4 - 1	7 - 0
8 - 1	10 - 5	9 - 4
10 - 7	12 - 6	6 - 3

Time: _____

- -

Subtraction Facts

Name: _____

10 - 4 = _____   12 - 3 = _____   13   9
                                    -7   -5

12 - 6 = _____   7 - 1 = _____

14 - 5 = _____   9 - 6 = _____   18   6
                                    -9   -6

16 - 9 = _____   8 - 0 = _____

8 - 8 = _____   7 - 3 = _____   7   14
                                    -2   -7

9 - 2 = _____   11 - 6 = _____

Time: _____

© Ideal School Supply • A Division of Instructional Fair Group, Inc.   Facts in a Flash: Addition & Subtraction, Grades 1-3 • ID7140

Addition Facts Cards

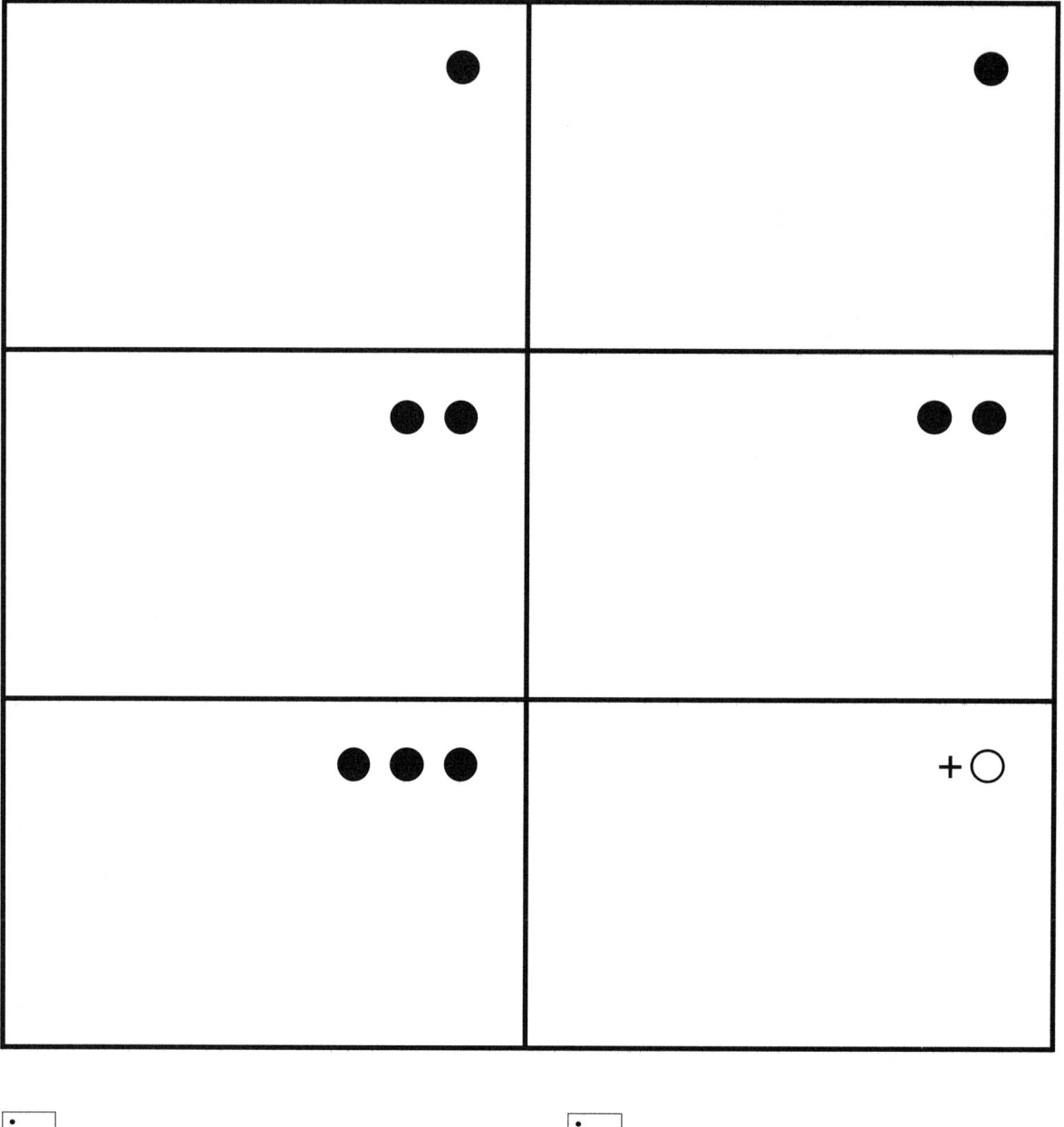

Counting-on 1 – 17 cards

Counting-on 2 – 14 cards

Counting-on 3 – 12 cards

Zero Property – 19 cards total

Addition Facts Cards

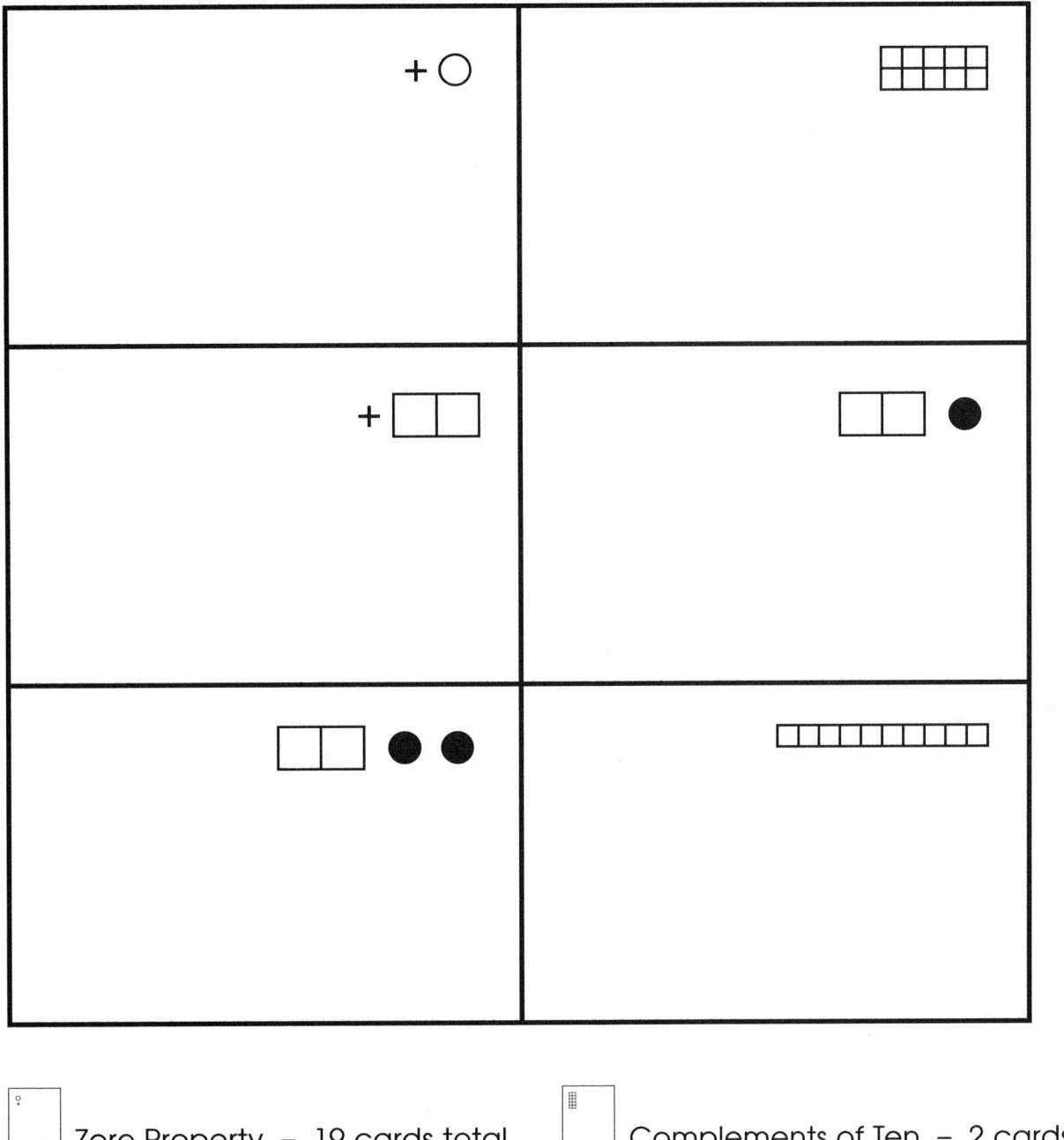

Zero Property – 19 cards total

Complements of Ten – 2 cards

Doubles – 6 cards

Doubles-Plus 1 – 10 cards

Doubles-Plus 2 – 6 cards

Make-a-Ten – 12 cards

Subtraction Facts Cards

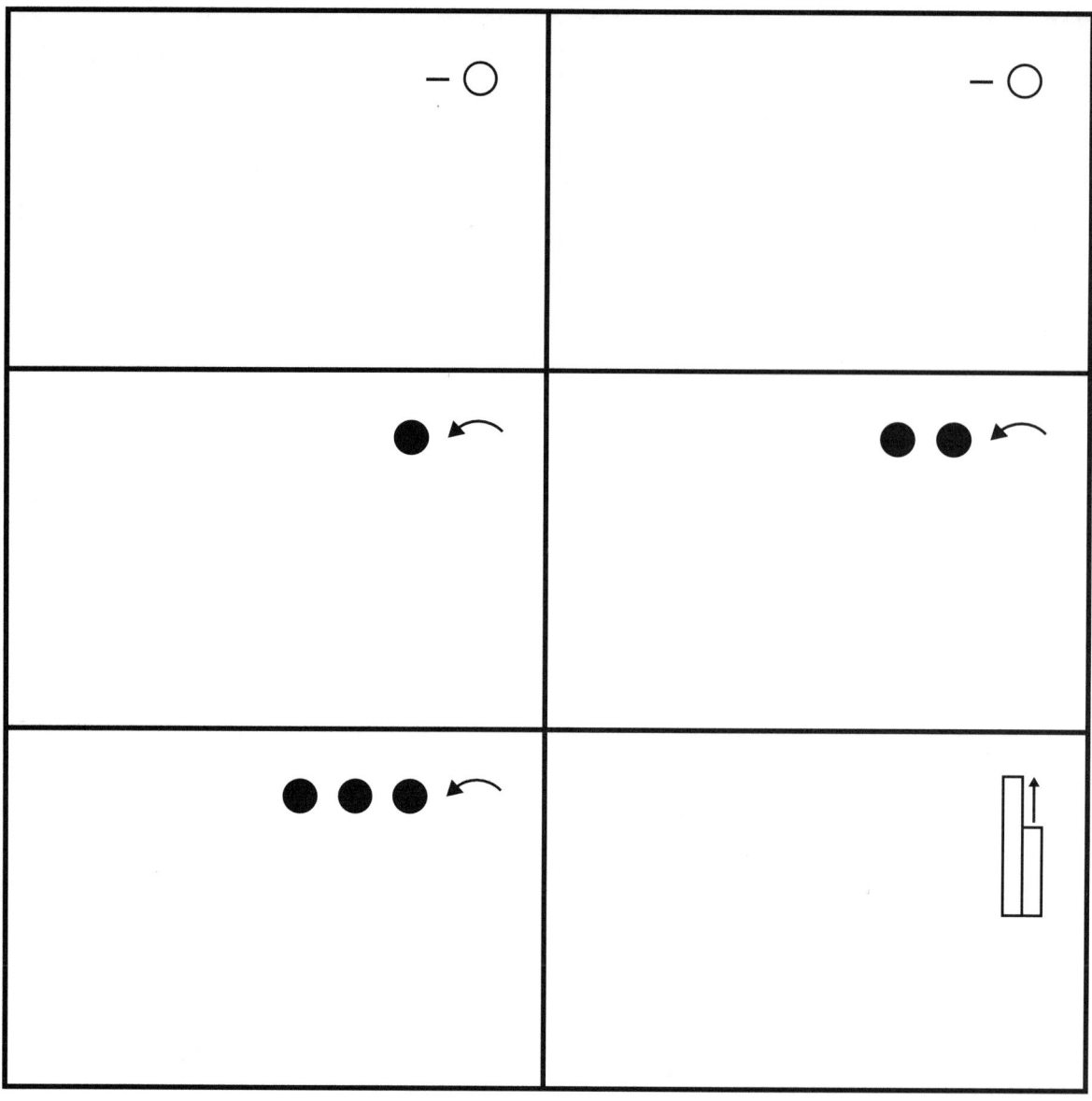

- Zero Property — 19 cards
- Counting Back 1 — 9 cards
- Counting Back 2 — 9 cards
- Counting Back 3 — 9 cards
- Counting Up — 18 cards total

Subtraction Facts Cards

Counting Up – 18 cards total

Doubles – 5 cards

Near Doubles – 10 cards

Use Addition – 20 cards

Cumulative Review I: Addition

Name: _____

0 + 1 = ____   3 + 3 = ____   5   6
                                  +0   +2
                                  ___   ___

4 + 3 = ____   9 + 9 = ____

8 + 8 = ____   3 + 2 = ____   8   5
                                  +9   +5
                                  ___   ___

7 + 2 = ____   2 + 1 = ____

6 + 4 = ____   7 + 7 = ____   7   6
                                  +8   +5
                                  ___   ___

9 + 1 = ____   8 + 2 = ____

Time: _____

- -

Cumulative Review II: Addition

Name: _____

4 + 4 = ____   9 + 1 = ____   8   2
                                  +4   +8
                                  ___   ___

7 + 5 = ____   6 + 6 = ____

3 + 5 = ____   9 + 8 = ____   5   7
                                  +2   +9
                                  ___   ___

4 + 6 = ____   5 + 5 = ____

7 + 4 = ____   5 + 6 = ____   9   8
                                  +6   +7
                                  ___   ___

3 + 9 = ____   6 + 8 = ____

Time: _____

Cumulative Review I: Subtraction

Name: _____

2 − 1 = ____   4 − 4 = ____   5   8
                                       −4   −7
                                       ___   ___

10 − 2 = ____   6 − 2 = ____

6 − 0 = ____   10 − 1 = ____   10   10
                                       −7   −8
                                       ___   ___

11 − 8 = ____   8 − 4 = ____

11 − 9 = ____   9 − 1 = ____   16   12
                                       −8   −6
                                       ___   ___

10 − 5 = ____   14 − 7 = ____

Time: _____

- -

Cumulative Review II: Subtraction

Name: _____

9 − 9 = ____   10 − 7 = ____   16   14
                                       −7   −9
                                       ___   ___

12 − 6 = ____   11 − 5 = ____

8 − 1 = ____   13 − 7 = ____   15   10
                                       −6   −4
                                       ___   ___

5 − 2 = ____   9 − 7 = ____

6 − 3 = ____   13 − 9 = ____   14   18
                                       −7   −9
                                       ___   ___

11 − 9 = ____   15 − 8 = ____

Time: _____

Mixed Review I

Name: _____

9 + 1 = ____   5 - 4 = ____   8   7
                                 +8   -1
                                 ___   ___

6 - 3 = ____   2 + 8 = ____

9 - 2 = ____   3 - 3 = ____   3   7
                                 +3   -3
                                 ___   ___

10 - 5 = ____   6 + 3 = ____

12 - 6 = ____   8 - 6 = ____   8   16
                                 -4   -8
                                 ___   ___

6 + 6 = ____   12 - 7 = ____

Time: _____

- -

Mixed Review II

Name: _____

15 - 9 = ____   5 + 4 = ____   13   6
                                 -6   +7
                                 ___   ___

9 + 4 = ____   11 - 5 = ____

4 + 5 = ____   15 - 7 = ____   8   17
                                 +5   -9
                                 ___   ___

3 + 8 = ____   10 - 8 = ____

6 + 9 = ____   16 - 8 = ____   9   15
                                 +7   -8
                                 ___   ___

9 + 5 = ____   14 - 8 = ____

Time: _____

Turnaround Facts Review I

Name: _____

4 + 5 = ____		9 + 4 = ____		14		5
							−6		+6
							———		———
13 − 7 = ____		15 − 8 = ____

8 + 4 = ____		6 + 8 = ____		 9		 7
							−5		+6
							———		———
11 − 5 = ____		13 − 4 = ____

9 + 6 = ____		7 + 4 = ____		12		 8
							−8		+7
							———		———
11 − 7 = ____		15 − 6 = ____

Time: _____

- -

Turnaround Facts Review II

Name: _____

8 + 4 = ____		5 + 7 = ____		16		17
							−9		−8
							———		———
11 − 7 = ____		17 − 9 = ____

6 + 7 = ____		9 + 5 = ____		 8		14
							+7		−5
							———		———
12 − 7 = ____		16 − 7 = ____

9 + 8 = ____		9 + 7 = ____		13		 4
							−7		+7
							———		———
15 − 7 = ____		12 − 4 = ____

Time: _____

Oral Facts Review

Children must not only learn a facts strategy, they must practice it until they are able to easily recall and use the strategy to name the facts quickly and correctly. To encourage fluency in basic facts, you might give children a weekly oral drill of up to ten facts. Ask fact questions that require use of one of the strategies such as: *What is one more than six? What is double fives? What is eight less four?* Such questions ensure that students practice the thinking required to accomplish fast recall of the facts.

Sample questions are provided for addition and subtraction facts. Make up additional review questions as needed. Students can write the operation and strategy being practiced on the top of lined paper as an answer sheet.

Addition Review

Counting-on Review

What is 1 more than 9? (10)
What is 7 plus 1? (8)
What is 2 more than 4? (6)
What is 2 more than 9? (11)
What is 3 more than 5? (9)
What is 2 more than 8? (10)
What is 3 plus 8? (11)
What is 2 plus 6? (8)
What is 3 more than 6? (9)
What is 2 more than 7? (9)

Doubles and Doubles-Plus Review

What is double 2? (4)
What is double 3? (6)
What is double 3 plus 1? (7)
What is double 7? (14)
What is double 8 plus 1? (9)
What is double 4? (8)
What is double 4 plus 1? (9)
What is double 5? (10)
What is double 5 plus 1? (11)
What is double 6? (12)

Make-a-Ten

What is 4 more than 7? (11)
What is 5 more than 9? (14)
What is 5 more than 8? (13)
What is 6 more than 9? (15)
What is 4 more than 9? (13)
What is 8 plus 4? (12)
What is 9 plus 6? (15)
What is 8 plus 5? (13)
What is 3 more than 8? (11)
What is 7 more than 9? (16)

Mixed Addition Facts

What is double 5? (10)
What is 3 more than 6? (9)
What is 4 more than 9? (13)
What is 2 more than 3? (5)
What is 5 more than 7? (12)
What is 8 more than 9? (17)
What is double 8? (16)
What is 2 more than 9? (11)
What is 3 plus 0? (3)
What is 3 more than 8? (11)

Subtraction Review

Counting Back

What is 1 less than 4? (3)
What is 3 less than 5? (2)
What is 2 less than 9? (7)
What is 1 less than 3? (2)
What is 2 less than 7? (5)
What is 3 less than 4? (1)
What is 2 less than 8? (6)
What is 3 less than 9? (6)
What is 1 less than 2? (1)
What is 3 less than 11? (8)

Counting Up

What is the difference between 5 and 4? (1)
What is the difference between 9 and 7? (2)
What is the difference between 11 and 9? (2)
What is the difference between 6 and 5? (1)
What is the difference between 10 and 7? (3)
What is the difference between 9 and 6? (3)
What is the difference between 10 and 9? (1)
What is the difference between 7 and 5? (2)
What is the difference between 8 and 5? (3)
What is the difference between 7 and 4? (3)

Doubles and Near Doubles

What is 8 minus 4? (4)
What is 12 minus 6? (6)
What is 14 minus 7? (7)
What is 17 minus 9? (8)
What is 16 minus 8? (8)
What is 13 minus 6? (7)
What is 11 minus 5? (6)
What is 10 minus 5? (5)
What is 9 minus 5? (4)
What is 17 minus 8? (9)

Use Addition

What is 11 minus 4? (7)
What is 16 minus 9? (7)
What is 12 minus 5? (7)
What is 14 minus 5? (9)
What is 11 minus 7? (4)
What is 13 minus 4? (9)
What is 15 minus 9? (6)
What is 10 minus 6? (4)
What is 12 minus 7? (5)
What is 16 minus 7? (9)

Selected Solutions

These are sample solutions. Additional answers are possible for some activities.

page 24

Counting-on

6 + 2 = 8	8 + 2 = 10	6 +2 / 8	3 +5 / 8
9 + 3 = 12	1 + 4 = 5	2 +4 / 6	1 +6 / 7
1 + 7 = 8	6 + 2 = 8		
2 + 4 = 6	7 + 1 = 8	8 +3 / 11	7 +2 / 9
6 + 3 = 9	2 + 8 = 10		
5 + 2 = 7	9 + 1 = 10		

Doubles

4 + 4 = 8	1 + 1 = 2	5 +5 / 10	9 +9 / 18
3 + 3 = 6	8 + 8 = 16	3 +3 / 6	7 +7 / 14
7 + 7 = 14	3 + 3 = 6		
6 + 6 = 12	9 + 9 = 18	8 +8 / 16	2 +2 / 4
2 + 2 = 4	6 + 6 = 12		
5 + 5 = 10	7 + 7 = 14		

page 22

Dora's Dots

What happens when Mary folds each dot picture?
Draw and write the doubles facts she makes.

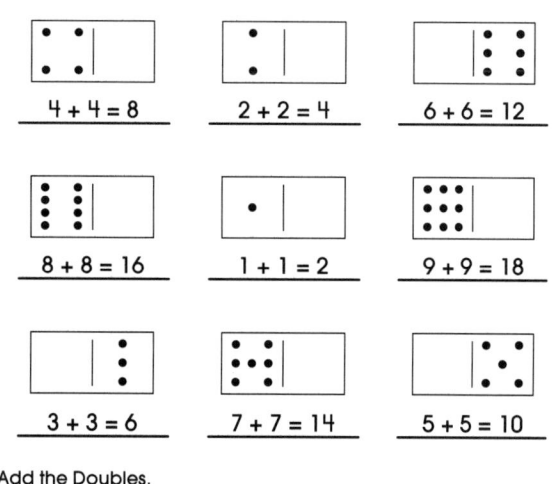

4 + 4 = 8   2 + 2 = 4   6 + 6 = 12
8 + 8 = 16   1 + 1 = 2   9 + 9 = 18
3 + 3 = 6   7 + 7 = 14   5 + 5 = 10

Add the Doubles.

1	2	3	4	5	6	7	8	9
+1	+2	+3	+4	+5	+6	+7	+8	+9
2	4	6	8	10	12	14	16	18

What pattern do you see? The pattern is skip counting by 2s; all the sums are even

page 25

Brenda's Blocks

Brenda has a bag of 10 yellow and blue blocks.
What could her collection look like?
Draw 4 different groups of 10 blocks.
Write a number sentence for the blocks in each bag.

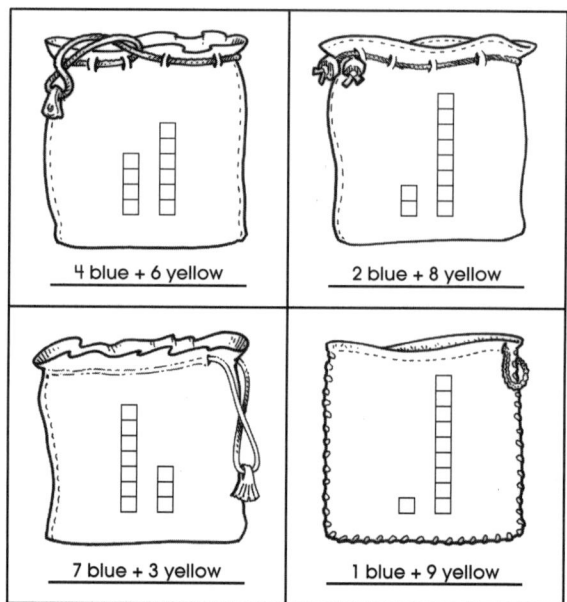

4 blue + 6 yellow   2 blue + 8 yellow
7 blue + 3 yellow   1 blue + 9 yellow

page 26

String Bead Sums

Sammy has string beads just like you. But some of his fell off!
Draw the beads to show 10 altogether.
Write the fact.

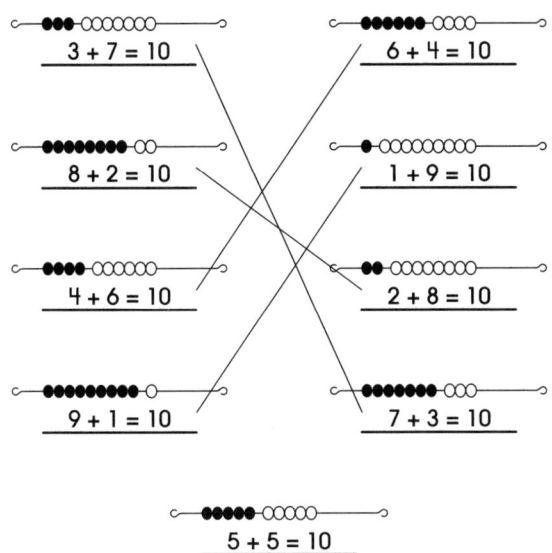

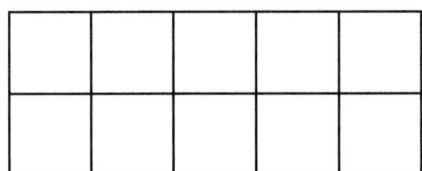

Draw a line to connect each turnaround fact.

page 27

Ten-Frame Facts

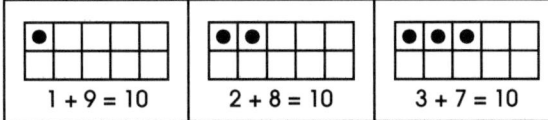

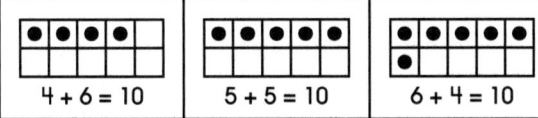

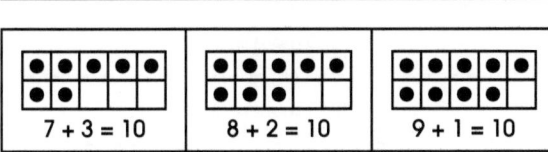

page 28

Totally Ten!

Name the parts of the tens bars.

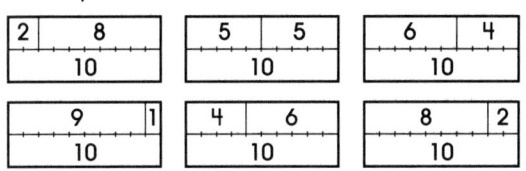

Name the missing part.
The tens bars can help you.

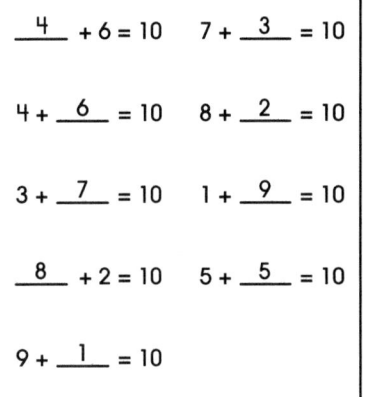

Match to make ten!

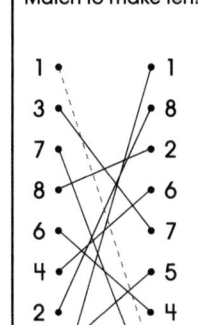

page 29

One More Dot!

Help Mary put a sticky dot on Dora's Doubles pictures.
Draw a dot on each picture.
Write the Doubles + 1 fact that you made.

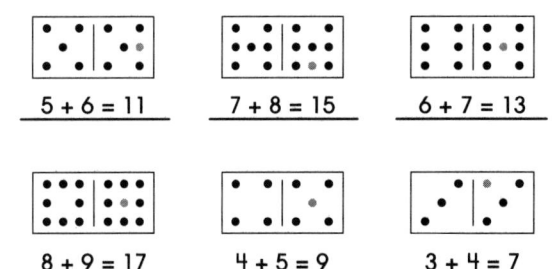

Doubles + 1 Dot to Dot

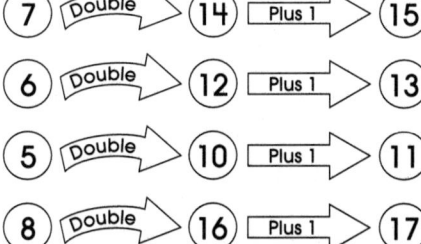

page 30

Helping Double

For each fact, write the helping double.
Then add 1 more to name each sum.

Fact	Helping Double	+ 1	Sum
5 + 6	5 + 5	+ 1	11
3 + 4	3 + 3	+ 1	7
8 + 7	7 + 7	+ 1	15
7 + 6	6 + 6	+ 1	13
4 + 3	3 + 3	+ 1	7
8 + 9	8 + 8	+ 1	17
4 + 5	4 + 4	+ 1	9
6 + 7	6 + 6	+ 1	13
6 + 5	5 + 5	+ 1	11
9 + 8	8 + 8	+ 1	17
5 + 4	4 + 4	+ 1	9

page 33

Doubles-Plus-One (Review)

4 + 5 = 9   7 + 6 = 13   6   7
6 + 7 = 13   9 + 8 = 17   +5   +6
3 + 2 = 5   3 + 4 = 7   11   13
4 + 3 = 7   7 + 8 = 15   9   5
8 + 9 = 17   5 + 6 = 11   +8   +6
5 + 4 = 9   8 + 7 = 15   17   11
                                 7   4
                                +8   +5
                                15   9

Doubles-Plus-Two (Review)

5 + 7 = 12   6 + 4 = 10   9   5
6 + 8 = 14   7 + 5 = 12   +7   +7
7 + 9 = 16   3 + 5 = 8   16   12
8 + 6 = 14   5 + 7 = 12   8   7
4 + 6 = 10   6 + 8 = 14   +6   +9
9 + 7 = 16   7 + 9 = 16   14   16
                                 7   6
                                +5   +8
                                12   14

page 32

Give and Take

This balance shows 6 + 4. Give...and take! Now it shows 5 + 5.

Balance each scale to make a double. Write the sum in the △.

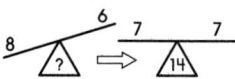 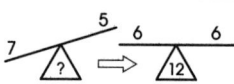

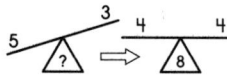 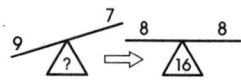

Find each Hidden Double and write the sum.

Fact	Hidden Double	Sum
8 + 6	7 + 7	14
6 + 4	5 + 5	10
5 + 7	6 + 6	12
9 + 7	8 + 8	16
6 + 8	7 + 7	14
7 + 5	6 + 6	12

page 34

Where's the Ten?

Where is the 10 hiding in each fact?
Write the numbers you think of to name each sum.

8 + 5   8 and 2 is 10. 3 more is 13.
         OR
         I know 5 + 5 is 10. 3 more is 13.

7 + 4   7 and 3 is 10. 1 more is 11. OR
         4 and 6 is 10. 1 more is 11.

4 + 8   8 and 2 is 10. 2 more is 12. OR
         4 and 6 is 10. 2 more is 12.

9 + 5   9 and 1 is 10. 4 more is 14. OR
         5 and 5 is 10. 4 more is 14.

4 + 7   7 and 3 is 10. 1 more is 11. OR
         4 and 6 is 10. 1 more is 11.

8 + 4   8 and 2 is 10. 2 more is 12. OR
         4 and 6 is 10. 2 more is 12.

6 + 9   9 and 1 is 10. 5 more is 15. OR
         6 and 4 is 10. 5 more is 15.

4 + 9   9 and 1 is 10. 3 more is 13. OR
         4 and 6 is 10. 3 more is 13.

page 35

Pondering Plus 9

Look for a pattern in the +9 facts.

$9 + 4 = 13 \quad 9 + 5 = 14 \quad 9 + 6 = 15$
$4 + 9 = 13 \quad 5 + 9 = 14 \quad 6 + 9 = 15$

Describe the pattern you see in the addends and the sum.

The sum of the two digits in the answer equals the smaller addend. Example: $4 + 9 = 13 \quad 1 + 3 = 4$ OR
The ones digit in the sum is one less than the smaller addend. Example: $9 + 6 = 15$

Use the pattern to help you write the missing addend or sum.

$9 + 5 = \underline{14}$ $\qquad$ $7 + 9 = \underline{16}$

$\underline{4} + 9 = 13$ $\qquad$ $9 + \underline{8} = 17$

$9 + \underline{7} = 16$ $\qquad$ $\underline{6} + 9 = 15$

$\underline{6} + 9 = 15$ $\qquad$ $9 + 4 = \underline{13}$

$8 + 9 = \underline{17}$ $\qquad$ $9 + \underline{5} = 14$

page 36

Make-a-Ten

$7 + 4 = \underline{11}$ $\quad$ $5 + 8 = \underline{13}$ $\quad$ $\begin{array}{r}6\\+9\\\hline 15\end{array}$ $\quad$ $\begin{array}{r}4\\+8\\\hline 12\end{array}$

$9 + 4 = \underline{13}$ $\quad$ $9 + 6 = \underline{15}$ $\quad$ $\begin{array}{r}5\\+8\\\hline 13\end{array}$ $\quad$ $\begin{array}{r}9\\+4\\\hline 13\end{array}$

$4 + 8 = \underline{12}$ $\quad$ $5 + 9 = \underline{14}$

$9 + 5 = \underline{14}$ $\quad$ $8 + 4 = \underline{12}$

$8 + 5 = \underline{13}$ $\quad$ $4 + 9 = \underline{13}$ $\quad$ $\begin{array}{r}9\\+5\\\hline 14\end{array}$ $\quad$ $\begin{array}{r}7\\+4\\\hline 11\end{array}$

$6 + 9 = \underline{15}$ $\quad$ $4 + 7 = \underline{11}$

Mixed Addition Facts

$4 + 4 = \underline{8}$ $\quad$ $2 + 9 = \underline{11}$ $\quad$ $\begin{array}{r}5\\+7\\\hline 12\end{array}$ $\quad$ $\begin{array}{r}8\\+6\\\hline 14\end{array}$

$6 + 3 = \underline{9}$ $\quad$ $6 + 6 = \underline{12}$

$7 + 5 = \underline{12}$ $\quad$ $5 + 3 = \underline{8}$ $\quad$ $\begin{array}{r}9\\+4\\\hline 13\end{array}$ $\quad$ $\begin{array}{r}8\\+8\\\hline 16\end{array}$

$1 + 9 = \underline{10}$ $\quad$ $7 + 6 = \underline{13}$

$8 + 7 = \underline{15}$ $\quad$ $8 + 9 = \underline{17}$ $\quad$ $\begin{array}{r}7\\+4\\\hline 11\end{array}$ $\quad$ $\begin{array}{r}5\\+2\\\hline 7\end{array}$

$6 + 5 = \underline{11}$ $\quad$ $9 + 6 = \underline{15}$

page 40

Counting Back

$6 - 2 = \underline{4}$ $\quad$ $9 - 3 = \underline{6}$ $\quad$ $\begin{array}{r}8\\-2\\\hline 6\end{array}$ $\quad$ $\begin{array}{r}7\\-1\\\hline 6\end{array}$

$7 - 3 = \underline{4}$ $\quad$ $6 - 2 = \underline{4}$

$8 - 1 = \underline{7}$ $\quad$ $5 - 4 = \underline{1}$ $\quad$ $\begin{array}{r}6\\-1\\\hline 5\end{array}$ $\quad$ $\begin{array}{r}5\\-3\\\hline 2\end{array}$

$3 - 1 = \underline{2}$ $\quad$ $7 - 2 = \underline{5}$

$5 - 2 = \underline{3}$ $\quad$ $9 - 2 = \underline{7}$ $\quad$ $\begin{array}{r}4\\-2\\\hline 2\end{array}$ $\quad$ $\begin{array}{r}2\\-1\\\hline 1\end{array}$

$6 - 3 = \underline{3}$ $\quad$ $8 - 3 = \underline{5}$

Zero Property

$5 - 5 = \underline{0}$ $\quad$ $2 - 0 = \underline{2}$ $\quad$ $\begin{array}{r}9\\-9\\\hline 0\end{array}$ $\quad$ $\begin{array}{r}8\\-0\\\hline 8\end{array}$

$6 - 0 = \underline{6}$ $\quad$ $1 - 1 = \underline{0}$

$3 - 3 = \underline{0}$ $\quad$ $4 - 4 = \underline{0}$ $\quad$ $\begin{array}{r}6\\-6\\\hline 0\end{array}$ $\quad$ $\begin{array}{r}5\\-0\\\hline 5\end{array}$

$5 - 0 = \underline{5}$ $\quad$ $7 - 0 = \underline{7}$

$4 - 0 = \underline{4}$ $\quad$ $8 - 8 = \underline{0}$ $\quad$ $\begin{array}{r}3\\-0\\\hline 3\end{array}$ $\quad$ $\begin{array}{r}2\\-2\\\hline 0\end{array}$

$7 - 7 = \underline{0}$ $\quad$ $9 - 0 = \underline{9}$

page 42

Drops on Doubles

Oops! As Ray was painting the clubhouse, he spilled white paint on his Doubles homework. Help Ray finish his homework. Write the numbers over the "paint" to complete each number sentence.

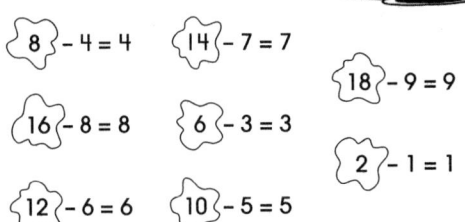

$\boxed{8} - 4 = 4$ $\quad$ $\boxed{14} - 7 = 7$

$\boxed{18} - 9 = 9$

$\boxed{16} - 8 = 8$ $\quad$ $\boxed{6} - 3 = 3$

$\boxed{2} - 1 = 1$

$\boxed{12} - 6 = 6$ $\quad$ $\boxed{10} - 5 = 5$

$12 - \boxed{6} = 6$ $\quad$ $10 - \boxed{5} = 5$

$8 - \boxed{4} = 4$ $\quad$ $18 - \boxed{9} = 9$

$\begin{array}{r}4\\-\boxed{2}\\\hline 2\end{array}$ $\quad$ $\begin{array}{r}16\\-\boxed{8}\\\hline 8\end{array}$ $\quad$ $\begin{array}{r}6\\-\boxed{3}\\\hline 3\end{array}$ $\quad$ $\begin{array}{r}14\\-\boxed{7}\\\hline 7\end{array}$

page 43

Counting Up

8 − 6 = 2	6 − 4 = 2	10 −7 = 3	11 −9 = 2
9 − 7 = 2	7 − 6 = 1	9 −8 = 1	10 −9 = 1
7 − 4 = 3	6 − 5 = 1		
5 − 4 = 1	8 − 5 = 3	7 −5 = 2	6 −4 = 2
7 − 5 = 2	9 − 6 = 3		
9 − 8 = 1	8 − 7 = 1		

Doubles

8 − 4 = 4	10 − 5 = 5	8 −4 = 4	10 −5 = 5
6 − 3 = 3	18 − 9 = 9	18 −9 = 9	16 −8 = 8
10 − 5 = 5	6 − 3 = 3		
4 − 2 = 2	16 − 8 = 8	14 −7 = 7	12 −6 = 6
14 − 7 = 7	12 − 6 = 6		
2 − 1 = 1	14 − 7 = 7		

page 44

Helping Doubles II

Match each Near Double with a Double that helps you name it.

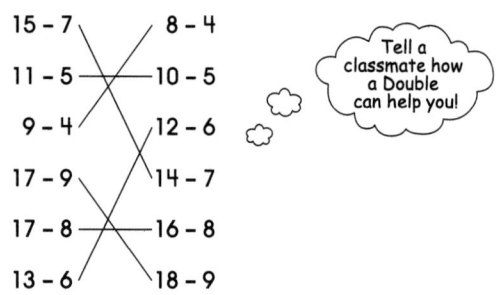

15 − 7 — 8 − 4
11 − 5 — 10 − 5
9 − 4 — 12 − 6
17 − 9 — 14 − 7
17 − 8 — 16 − 8
13 − 6 — 18 − 9

Tell a classmate how a Double can help you!

How do you know each difference?
Write about your thinking.

11 − 6   12 − 6 is 6, 11 is one less, so it's 5. Check: 5 + 6 = 11

9 − 5   10 − 5 is 5, 9 is one less, so it's 4. Check: 4 + 5 = 9

13 − 7   14 − 7 is 7, 13 is one less, so it's 6. Check: 6 + 7 = 13

17 − 9   18 − 9 is 9, 17 is one less, so it's 8. Check: 8 + 9 = 17

page 45

Missing Part Puzzles

Write the missing part.
Write each addition fact and the subtraction fact for each box.

5	6
11	

5 + 6 = 11
11 − 5 = 6

6	2
8	

6 + 2 = 8
8 − 2 = 6

9	6
15	

9 + 6 = 15
15 − 9 = 6

5	9
14	

5 + 9 = 14
14 − 5 = 9

7	5
12	

7 + 5 = 12
12 − 7 = 5

9	7
16	

9 + 7 = 16
16 − 7 = 9

5	8
13	

5 + 8 = 13
13 − 5 = 8

7	4
11	

7 + 4 = 11
11 − 7 = 4

6	8
14	

6 + 8 = 14
14 − 8 = 6

Make your own.

Answers will vary.

page 46

Near Doubles

9 − 4 = 5	9 − 5 = 4	17 −8 = 9	11 −6 = 5
11 − 5 = 6	15 − 8 = 7		
17 − 8 = 9	11 − 6 = 5	15 −8 = 7	13 −6 = 7
13 − 6 = 7	13 − 7 = 6		
15 − 7 = 8	11 − 5 = 6	13 −7 = 6	9 −5 = 4
17 − 9 = 8	9 − 4 = 5		

Use Addition

12 − 8 = 4	11 − 7 = 4	13 −4 = 9	15 −9 = 6
14 − 5 = 9	13 − 8 = 5		
12 − 4 = 8	16 − 9 = 7	10 −6 = 4	14 −6 = 8
14 − 9 = 5	16 − 7 = 9		
13 − 5 = 8	13 − 9 = 4	10 −4 = 6	12 −7 = 5
11 − 4 = 7	15 − 6 = 9		

page 47

Subtraction Facts

Match 3 facts that have the same difference.

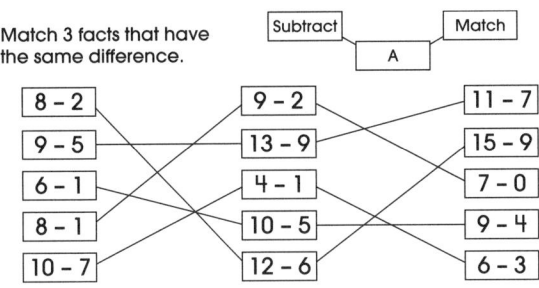

Subtraction Facts

10 - 4 = 6   12 - 3 = 9   13-7=6   9-5=4
12 - 6 = 6   7 - 1 = 8
14 - 5 = 9   9 - 6 = 3   18-9=9   6-6=0
16 - 9 = 7   8 - 0 = 8
8 - 8 = 0   7 - 3 = 4   7-2=5   14-7=7
9 - 2 = 7   11 - 6 = 5

page 52

Cumulative Review I: Addition

0 + 1 = 1   3 + 3 = 6   5+0=5   6+2=8
4 + 3 = 7   9 + 9 = 18
8 + 8 = 16   3 + 2 = 5   8+9=17   5+5=10
7 + 2 = 9   2 + 1 = 3
6 + 4 = 10   7 + 7 = 14   7+8=15   6+5=11
9 + 1 = 10   8 + 2 = 10

Cumulative Review II: Addition

4 + 4 = 8   9 + 1 = 10   8+4=12   2+8=10
7 + 5 = 12   6 + 6 = 12
3 + 5 = 8   9 + 8 = 17   5+2=7   7+9=16
4 + 6 = 10   5 + 5 = 10
7 + 4 = 11   5 + 6 = 11   9+6=15   8+7=15
3 + 9 = 12   6 + 8 = 14

page 53

Cumulative Review I: Subtraction

2 - 1 = 1   4 - 4 = 0   5-4=1   8-7=1
10 - 2 = 8   6 - 2 = 4
6 - 0 = 6   10 - 1 = 9   10-7=3   10-8=2
11 - 8 = 3   8 - 4 = 4
11 - 9 = 2   9 - 1 = 8   16-8=8   12-6=6
10 - 5 = 5   14 - 7 = 7

Cumulative Review II: Subtraction

9 - 9 = 0   10 - 7 = 3   16-7=9   14-9=5
12 - 6 = 6   11 - 5 = 6
8 - 1 = 7   13 - 7 = 6   15-6=9   10-4=6
5 - 2 = 3   9 - 7 = 2
6 - 3 = 3   13 - 9 = 4   14-7=7   18-9=9
11 - 9 = 2   15 - 8 = 7

page 54

Mixed Review I

9 + 1 = 10   5 - 4 = 1   8+8=16   7-1=6
6 - 3 = 3   2 + 8 = 10
9 - 2 = 7   3 - 3 = 0   3+3=6   7-3=4
10 - 5 = 5   6 + 3 = 9
12 - 6 = 6   8 - 6 = 2   8-4=4   16-8=8
6 + 6 = 12   12 - 7 = 5

Mixed Review II

15 - 9 = 6   5 + 4 = 9   13-6=7   6+7=13
9 + 4 = 13   11 - 5 = 6
4 + 5 = 9   15 - 7 = 8   8+5=13   17-9=8
3 + 8 = 11   10 - 8 = 2
6 + 9 = 15   16 - 8 = 8   9+7=16   15-8=7
9 + 5 = 14   14 - 8 = 6

page 55

Turnaround Facts Review I

4 + 5 = __9__   9 + 4 = __13__   14   5
                                     −6   +6
13 − 7 = __6__   15 − 8 = __7__   ――   ――
                                      8   11

8 + 4 = __12__   6 + 8 = __14__   9   7
                                     −5   +6
11 − 5 = __6__   13 − 4 = __9__   ――   ――
                                      4   13

9 + 6 = __15__   7 + 4 = __11__   12   8
                                     −8   +7
11 − 7 = __4__   15 − 6 = __9__   ――   ――
                                      4   15

- -

Turnaround Facts Review II

8 + 4 = __12__   5 + 7 = __12__   16   17
                                     −9   −8
11 − 7 = __4__   17 − 9 = __8__   ――   ――
                                      7   9

6 + 7 = __13__   9 + 5 = __14__   8   14
                                     +7   −5
12 − 7 = __5__   16 − 7 = __9__   ――   ――
                                     15   9

9 + 8 = __17__   9 + 7 = __16__   13   4
                                     −7   +7
15 − 7 = __8__   12 − 4 = __8__   ――   ――
                                      6   11